Michael L

Seasons and Feasts of the Church Year

An Introduction

PAULIST PRESS
New York/Mahwah, N.J.

The hymns used in this book are taken from *The Resource Collection of Hymns and Service Music for the Liturgy,* "Hymns in the Public Domain," published by GIA Publications, Inc., © 1981. All hymns are used with the permission of the International Committee on English in the Liturgy, Inc. (ICEL).

Copyright © 1993 by Michael D. Whalen

Library of Congress Cataloging-in-Publication Data

Whalen, Michael D.
    Seasons and feasts of the church year: an introduction/Michael D. Whalen.
      p. cm.
    Includes bibliographical references and index.
    ISBN 0-8091-3346-6 (paper)
    1. Church year. 2. Catholic Church—Liturgy. I. Title.
  BV30.W48   1992
  263'.9—dc20
                                              92-24215
                                                 CIP

Published by Paulist Press
997 Macarthur Boulevard
Mahwah, New Jersey 07430

Printed and bound in the United States of America

Contents

*To my mother, Doris, resting in
the peace of God,
and my father, John,*

*thank you both for a glimpse of
God's maternal and paternal
face.*

Preface

At the outset a word is in order about the intended purpose of and audience for this book. It has been written primarily as an introduction to the liturgical year for Roman Catholics who have had little or no formal schooling in liturgiology, especially the liturgical year. Thus, among those who might find this book helpful are parish liturgical ministers, religious educators, catechumens, and the many Roman Catholics who seek to understand the liturgy more deeply, yet do not (and need not) possess a graduate degree in matters liturgical. Those who have been professionally trained in liturgy as a discipline might also find this work helpful, though they will undoubtedly be familiar with what is contained here. Because of the common shape of the liturgical year among various Christian denominations, those not within the Roman Catholic tradition might also find this work useful and interesting.

Throughout the book attention has been paid to the historical development, the theological meaning (though this is hard to nail down at times), and the pastoral issues involved in the celebration of the feasts and seasons of the liturgical year. The historical development presented herein has sought to respect and present points of consensus which have been reached by scholars in this field. Technical and hypothetical issues have been avoided for the most part. The theological meanings presented have sought to respect the polyvalence of liturgy, involving as it does both symbol and ritual, always accompanied by a rich surplus of meaning. The pastoral issues presented are those about which questions are often raised by those who prepare liturgy, the faithful at large, and newcomers to the Roman Catholic Church.

More importantly, it is hoped that this book will provide the

1

tone and spirit of the church's cycle of seasons and feasts. In many respects the primary concern throughout the text has been to provide a method for understanding, preparing for, and celebrating Christian seasons and feasts. While concrete pastoral issues have been discussed the text makes no pretense of settling such issues definitively.

Of course, no book simply writes itself—and a few heartfelt "thank yous" are in order. I wish to thank the various novice classes of the Eastern Province of the Vincentians; the parishioners of St. John Bosco Parish, Hatboro, Pennsylvania; and the "Liturgical Year" class of La Salle University's 1990 Summer Session. All have served as "editors" of this work in one way or another. I also wish to acknowledge and thank Sister Catherine Dooley, Ph.D., and Father C. Gerard Austin, S.T.D. Sister Dooley's thoughts on liturgical catechesis and Father Austin's thoughts on the liturgical year helped give shape to the ideas contained here. I wish to thank my confrere and friend, Joseph A. Morris, C.M. In many respects his thoughts on the liturgy have served as "the ants in the pants" of many ideas in this book. I also need to thank Mark E. Hartman. Several years ago when I began to give meager presentations on the liturgical year, he suggested that I eventually convert my thoughts and notes into a book. I hope this book is worthy of that suggestion.

Last, but certainly not least, I must thank Father Kevin W. Irwin, S.T.D., of The Catholic University of America. Father Irwin is the main catalyst behind this book and has offered a number of helpful criticisms along the way. I only hope that this book will do a tiny bit of justice to all I have learned from him and my other professors at The Catholic University of America.

1

General Introduction to the Study of the Liturgical Year

I said to the man at the gate of the year, "Give me a light that I may tread safely into the unknown." And he replied, "Go out into the darkness and put your hand into the hand of God. That shall be to you better than light and safer than a known way."

MINNIE LOUISE HASKINS

God looked at everything that God had made, and found it very good.

GENESIS 1:31

THE MYSTERY OF TIME

Time itself is sacred and good. Within time, however, some moments are experienced as freighted with thick meaning, and thus appear *more sacred*. Others are less so. We need these moments of the intense perception of time's meaning and sacredness to remind us of the sacredness of all time in itself.

It is sometimes said that in the liturgy one enters into "sacred time" in contrast to the "profane time" in which most of life is lived. Dividing time into categories of "sacred" and "profane," however, can lead to an unhealthy dichotomy. The use of such categories leads to a depreciation of the sacredness and goodness of time and creation in themselves. Certainly the "original blessing" to which the Genesis story points yields this foundational goodness and sacredness.

Such a perspective helps us to realize that time itself is a gift of grace and in the nature of ***sacrament.*** Furthermore, it helps us appre-

3

ciate the fundamental sacramentality of all time, which then grounds the sacramentality of liturgical time.

To understand this interpretation of time from a biblical perspective, a useful set of categories are *chronos* and *kairos*. *Chronos* is an interpretation of time which refers simply to its forward movement. Time is not an eternal return to the past (as sometimes understood by some mythic religions). It has a beginning and an end. Time stretches from Alpha to Omega, beginning to end, creation to judgment.

Kairos, on the other hand, involves dense and decisive points in time. *Kairos* is time thick with power and meaning. From a Christian perspective the *kairos* time par excellence is the paschal mystery of Jesus Christ, his passover from death to life, which the Christian community continues to reactualize in the liturgy. The celebrations of the liturgical year, therefore, are not "sacred times" (as opposed to "profane times"); rather, they are *kairos* time.

In the scriptures these *kairos* times are cosmic events, that is, the whole cosmos itself seems to be shaken, to respond. It is no accident that in the scriptures the heavens themselves announce the birth of Jesus Christ with a new star. Nor is it an accident that the earth is shaken and the sky is darkened when Christ dies. The cosmos senses *kairos* and responds.

Unfortunately, much of this cosmic sense has been lost as a result of the Enlightenment, the mechanization of time, and the process called "demythologization." Perhaps in this regard we are in need of a second naiveté. The rhythmic, melodic and enchanting tolling of a bell to announce time is a vastly different experience than a quick and isolated glance at a wristwatch. When people complain that liturgy no longer seems "sacred" it is often the blandness that results from mechanized time and runaway demythologization which is the problem.

THE MANY "TIMES" OF OUR LIVES

The notion of *kairos* time as cosmic event should not be too surprising. In many respects the "telling of time" is related to the cosmos. There are any number of aspects of time which are related to the movements of the sun and moon. The *year* relies on the movement of the earth in relation to the sun. The *month* relies on the movement of the moon in relation to the earth. The *day,* like the year, also relies on the movement of the earth on its axis, once again in relation to the sun.

There have also been (and are) varying ways by which the transition from one day to another has been marked. The Jewish people marked the day from sunset to sunset. The Greeks marked the day from dawn to dawn. The Romans marked the day from midnight to midnight.

The notion and calculation of the *week,* however, is a different matter. The week, though not simply arbitrary, is not related to the moon. Insofar as it involves a period of days, it has some relationship to the sun. But why *seven* days?

The actual origins of the week continue to remain obscure. The week is evidently unrelated to the cosmos in the sense that it can be "read" in the heavens. It appears to be the product of human calculation. In this sense it is more a matter of culture than cosmos—a *social convention.*

The Hebrew scriptures suggest that the week, interestingly enough, is a kind of *gift from God.* Throughout the Hebrew scriptures one also finds a certain prominence given to "7" as a number. For example, mourning periods lasted 7 days (Gen 50:10), Job was consoled by his friends for 7 days (Job 2:13), and long marches lasted 7 days (Gen 31:23). God, of course, also rested on the seventh day (Gen 2:1–3). In Babylonian thought, however, divisions of seven were thought to be evil. Thus, it could be the case that the Israelites were turning a pagan evil into an Israelite good.

When the Romans conquered the Jewish people they adopted and universalized the Jewish practice of a seven-day week (with its day of rest). However, the Romans named the different days after their gods.

We cannot ignore either the *day, month* and *year* as cosmic rhythms, or the *week* as social convention, because the liturgical years makes use of these. Elements of the liturgical year are rooted in a fixed calendar. For example, December 25 is a fixed celebration, as well as the accompanying Advent-Christmas-Epiphany cycle in which it occurs. Christmas is not dependent on a particular day of the week or on the lunar calendar. Other elements of the liturgical year are rooted in a movable calendar, for instance, the observance of the Pasch, as well as the Lent-Easter-Pentecost cycle which surrounds it. The Pasch is related to the lunar calendar and Easter is aligned with Sunday.

In addition to cosmic rhythms and times, persons and communities often operate within other given interpretations and experiences of time. Among these are: *biological time,* that is, a person's "body clock"; *cultural time,* that is, a marking of time which is specific to any given culture (for example, academic and fiscal calendar periods); *physical time,* that is, the telling of time by clocks; *personal time,* that is, the psychological state of a person; and so forth.

The point here is that people operate within a number of different experiences of time. Within the context of the liturgical year, it is important to note that these varying experiences of time cannot always (if ever) be isolated from one another. People may, do, and will bring these experiences of time with them to the celebrations of the liturgical year. For example, a person's biological time (tiredness) and personal time (depression) may affect her or his ability to enter into the celebrations of the liturgical year. The calendars around which people organize their lives must also be considered. Among some of these are: civil calendars, academic calendars, work calendars, commercial calendars (rooted in the purchasing of holiday items), and familial calendars (for example, birthdays and anniversaries).

THE PASCHAL MYSTERY: HEART OF THE LITURGICAL YEAR

The heart of the liturgical year (and every liturgical celebration within it) is the ***paschal mystery.*** In short, the term ***paschal mystery*** refers to the passion, death, resurrection and ascension of Jesus the Christ. No other Jesus is available to us. This, of course, does not ostensibly exclude the life of Jesus. Yet, there is an intricate relationship between the life of Jesus and his passion, death, resurrection and ascension. The meaning of Jesus' life most clearly emerges in and through the paschal mystery. Most of the texts of the liturgical year reflect our appropriation and experience of this paschal mystery.

The paschal mystery, however, is not simply a past event which we call to mind. Rather, it is the mystery of Christ's passion, death, resurrection and ascension into which we are drawn. The second (as well as the third and fourth) form of the acclamation of the "mystery of faith" which we proclaim during the eucharistic prayer reminds us of this:

> Dying you destroyed **our** death,
> rising you restored **our** life,
> Lord Jesus, come in glory!

There is a sense in which one can speak about two dimensions of the paschal mystery. On the one hand, the paschal mystery celebrates the passion, death, resurrection and ascension of Jesus Christ two thousand years ago. On the other hand, we are drawn into the paschal mystery which is made available to us in the liturgy.

THE LITURGICAL YEAR:
A CHRISTIAN UNDERSTANDING OF TIME

The liturgical year, in its cycles and feasts, celebrates a Christian understanding of time, which seeks to carefully hold in tensive balance time as an incarnational and eschatological reality.

On the one hand, the liturgical year is marked by a certain *incarnational* quality rooted in the theological principle of mediation. The Christian community takes seriously the affirmation that the disclosure of God is a possibility even **now.** This affirmation is enshrined in many of the liturgical texts. For example, the opening antiphon for the vigil mass of Christmas is: "*Today* you will know that the Lord is coming to save us, and in the morning you will see his glory." This antiphon is addressed to the gathered assembly. This "now-ness" is also brought out beautifully in the Easter proclamation (the Exsultet) through the repeated use of the phrase, *"This is the night. . . ."*

> This is the night when you first saved our ancestors:
> you freed the people of Israel from their slavery and
> led them dryshod through the sea.
> This is the night when Jesus Christ broke the chains
> of death and rose triumphant from the grave.

It is neither an exclusively past nor future event. It is an event which, though rooted in the past, is experienced in the present in such a way that the future is summoned.

The liturgical year is never simply a biography of Jesus of Nazareth or a celebration of past ecclesial events. Rather, it is the church's attempt to lay itself open to the memory of the Jesus story in such a way that the risen Christ is disclosed even now; and even now we experience salvation in and through the risen Christ. As a community we make memory by entering into the actuality of the Christ event which is made accessible through the liturgy. Christians are not Gnostics who are saved by a special knowledge of secret ideas, thoughts or themes. Our salvation is Jesus the Christ.

On the other hand, this incarnational quality is held in tension with an essentially eschatological thrust. The liturgical year does not simply celebrate the passage of time, nor does it simply celebrate the "now-ness" of redemption. The liturgical year is time toward. There is a sense in which we can speak of the *parousia* as a root metaphor of the liturgical year.

The liturgical year is sometimes imagined as a straight line moving forward, or a circle. Neither a straight line nor a circle, however, is the most appropriate way to illustrate the liturgical year. Perhaps the best way to image the liturgical year is by means of a forward moving or ascending spiral. Christians understand time to be moving forward in a way which is cognizant of past and present.

This forward or *eschatological* nature involves both a time "above" and a time "ahead." Liturgy is eschatological in that it is an entering into the heavenly liturgy which even now awaits us beyond death. (To maintain that "sacraments shall cease" beyond death is not to suggest that liturgy ceases.) This dimension of the liturgy's eschatological nature is expressed in that portion of the preface prayer which introduces the *sanctus.* This dynamic can be seen clearly in all of the prefaces for the Sundays in Ordinary Time:

> And so, with all the choirs of angels in heaven
> we proclaim your glory
> and join their unending hymn of praise:
> > *Preface I and II*

In many respects this dimension of the liturgy's eschatological underpinning has yet to take hold of western Christians, especially Roman Catholics. While we do sometimes consider the heavenly liturgy beyond the grave, we commonly fail to realize that even in the present we are drawn into the heavenly liturgy. We do not need to wait until death.

Another shade of this eschatological approach is the conviction that Jesus Christ will return in glory, although the actual interpretation of such a statement is difficult today. However, it is fair to suggest that the Christian community has generally sensed a certain element of absence vis-à-vis Jesus Christ. There is a sense in which Christ is present, yet paradoxically Christ is also absent. At one time churches were built to face east precisely because it was believed that Christ would return from the east.

However, lest liturgy become cultic self-preoccupation or powerless wishing, this time "above" must be balanced by a time "ahead" eschatology. That is, an understanding of liturgy which celebrates a new heaven and *new earth,* and which understands liturgy as a participation in the construction of a *new earth.* In this respect the liturgical year is eschatological in that it involves the Christian community in a kind of "grammar" of personal and social transformation. The liturgy is the arena in which we are transformed as individuals, yet it is also the place where the old world is transformed and a new world emerges. From a Christian perspective the liturgy is an important moment in the process of communal transformation. It celebrates and actualizes the dawn of a decisively new age which was inaugurated by Jesus.

THE LITURGICAL YEAR: GENERAL PRINCIPLES

Anamnesis. In the feasts and seasons of the liturgical year the church engages in an act of *anamnesis.* The liturgical year is not simply a matter of "remembering," as that term is commonly understood. As has been noted, in the liturgical year we neither repeat nor return to the past.

Anamnesis might best be described or defined as the reactualization of saving events in such a way that the past impinges on our present and moves us toward the future. In this sense one might speak about the liturgical year in terms of memory, presence and hope. This *anamnesis* is always a corporate or communal act of memory.

From a more critical perspective one must note that both *anamnesis* and corporate amnesia must be held in a healthy tension. What the Christian community remembers in the liturgy is of great importance; however, what the Christian community has forgotten is also of some import. For example, recent Christian feminist thought is reminding the Christian community that the memory of women has often been forgotten or distorted. (The issue of feminist liturgical anamnesis will be discussed briefly in chapter 2.)

Icon. The liturgical year is of its nature a "symbol" or "icon" of the Christian understanding of time. This principle pulls together and sums up much that has been said thus far. Among these dimensions are: 1) Jesus Christ is at the heart of the liturgical year; 2) Time involves past, present and future—all of these are important; 3) Time is a matter of movement forward toward the *parousia.*

The celebrations of the liturgical year are not simply the transcendence of time. Rather, they are the transformation of time. The liturgical year is time itself brought under the scrutiny of the gospel.

Here it must be acknowledged that for many people the liturgical year is hardly (if at all) experienced as an icon, sacrament, symbol—that is, as an opening into the mystery of God. More often than not there are complaints to the contrary—"There's no sense of mystery or sacredness about the liturgy." Time itself, however, is a kind of sacrament for the Christian—a sacrament of the mystery of existence itself, a sacrament of the mediatory activity of God, a sacrament of the sacredness of the entire cosmos. Paradoxically it is also a sacrament of the hiddenness of the mystery of God.

The liturgical year is a way of interpreting, organizing, marking time, and as such can be considered sacramental. Time itself is drawn into the redeeming work of Christ which took place and takes place in time, and which continues until time is no more, until "sacraments shall cease."

Furthermore, by virtue of extension the liturgical year can be considered **sacramental.** There is no such thing as the "liturgical year" in the abstract. The various cycles, feasts and days of the liturgical year are associated with "sacramentals." There abound throughout the liturgical year sacred signs which are bound to holy time. For example:

ashes—Ash Wednesday
palms—Palm Sunday
washing of feet—Holy Thursday
venerating the cross—Good Friday
blessing of throats—St. Blaise Day

These generally do not, and cannot, work at other times of the year.

The challenge which the liturgical year presents on a pastoral level is the transformation of the liturgical cycles into an experience in the "sacramentality of time."

Cosmos. The celebrations of the liturgical year are intimately linked to time as time has been and is experienced and interpreted through the cosmos. This sense of cosmos needs to be reappropriated within a twentieth-century context. Since different regions experience the cosmos differently, this varies from place to place. For our purposes we need to speak about an experience of the cosmos in a North American (and somewhat urban) context.

Transformation. It has already been noted that the celebrations of the liturgical year involve the ecclesial community in a kind of grammar of personal and social transformation. This mission orientation of the liturgical year is one which is sometimes overlooked. It needs, however, to be highlighted. For example, it may be no accident that the closing feasts of the Advent-Christmas-Epiphany cycle, the Lent-Easter-Pentecost cycle, and Ordinary Time can be interpreted as having strong mission orientations. The feasts of the Baptism of the Lord, Pentecost and Christ the King call people to transformation and mission.

Texts. In working out an appropriate theology of the liturgical year certain texts should be consulted. It often happens that the lectionary texts bear the burden for understanding the cycles and feasts of the liturgical year. However, there are a number of other texts which help uncover the meaning of any given cycle, feast or day within the liturgical year. These texts will be discussed in the final section of this chapter.

Rank. The liturgical year consists of individual celebrations which vary according to rank. Not all individual celebrations are of equal importance.

The *General Norms for the Liturgical Year and the Calendar* (hereafter GNLYC) designates these celebrations as: solemnities, feasts and memorials (#10). Memorials can be either "obligatory" or "optional." An obligatory memorial is one which must be celebrated; an optional memorial is one which may be celebrated.

Solemnities are the principal days in the calendar. Their liturgical importance is manifested in a number of ways. For example, the celebration of a solemnity begins with evening prayer on the preceding day. Some solemnities have special liturgical texts for use at the vigil mass (for example, Christmas, Easter, Pentecost, Assumption). Even among the solemnities themselves there is a certain hierarchy of importance. The chief among the solemnities are Christmas and Easter, both of which are accompanied by octave days (GNLYC #12, 13). These are the only two solemnities which have retained octave days in the reformed calendar.

Feasts are next in order of importance. As a rule, these are celebrated within the parameters of the natural twenty-four-hour day and do not usually have an evening prayer on the eve. The GNLYC notes that the exceptions to this rule are "feasts of the Lord that fall on a Sunday in Ordinary Time and in the Christmas season and that replace the Sunday office" (#13).

Memorials are least in order of importance. The celebration of these "is integrated into the celebration of the occurring weekday . . ." (GNLYC #14). Obligatory memorials are to be celebrated as a rule. However, obligatory memorials which occur on the weekdays of Lent may be celebrated as optional memorials.

Ecology. A proper ecology of Christian liturgy suggests that all liturgical celebrations have reference within the context of the liturgical year. The tendency exists to celebrate a number of liturgical rites as if they simply took place apart from the context of the liturgical year. For example, it is possible to celebrate the marriage rite during Advent-Christmas-Epiphany or Lent-Easter-Pentecost with no reference to the liturgical cycle in which the rite is situated.

Both liturgical directives and liturgical prayers, however, suggest that all liturgy takes place within the framework of the celebrations of the liturgical year. A few examples suffice here to make the point: The *Sacramentary* notes that, as a rule, the sacraments are not celebrated on Good Friday and Holy Saturday. Also, the rite for the ordination of a priest suggests that the ordination should take place on a Sunday or holy day. Finally, the directives for the rite of marriage state that when the marriage rite is celebrated during Advent, Lent, or special days of penance, the couple should take the special nature of these days into consideration.

There are other examples which could be offered here, but these few make the point adequately. The celebration of the various sacramental rites ought to be cognizant of the broader framework of the liturgical year within which such sacramental rites always take place. Weddings, burials and ordinations are never cut free of the liturgical year. They are situated within its framework.

THE LITURGICAL YEAR IS NOT . . .

Before undertaking a fuller examination and theology of the liturgical year it is helpful to clarify the mistaken notions about the liturgical year.

The liturgical year is not essentially a celebration of the biography of Jesus of Nazareth. A strict biography of Jesus of Nazareth per se is unavailable to us. The gospels are themselves not biographies. They are a distinct genre of literature written from a faith perspective.

The very structure of the liturgical year yields the insight that it is not a biography. Were the celebrations, feasts and seasons of the liturgical year simply a biography of Jesus, it would be logical to begin with the annunciation/nativity and conclude with the passion/death/resurrection/sending of the Spirit. However, in the present Roman Catholic liturgical year we find the following pattern: Advent-Christmas-Epiphany > Ordinary Time > Lent-Easter-Pentecost > Ordinary Time. The mainline Protestant denominations also employ a similar pattern.

Although it is not a biography of Jesus, the liturgical year does draw us into the "Jesus story." Thus, it has a certain narrative dimension.

The liturgical year is not a repetition of nor a return to past events, either in the personal life of Jesus or in the corporate story of the church. This is a different notion from a biography in that it is a type of pretense that "we are there." A repetition of or return to the past, however, is impossible. The past is the past. The liturgical year does not simply deal with history as that term is commonly understood. Rather, the liturgical year deals with tradition. The liturgical year is oriented to the past, present and future.

The liturgical year involves the memory and celebration of saving persons and events. These are unrepeatable yet remain available to us through the liturgical celebration which actualizes them in the present. These events perdure in the liturgy and continue to be a source of saving grace.

One is dealing here with both paradox and mystery. The liturgy is meta-historical, yet in history; trans-temporal, yet in time.

The liturgical year is not a celebration of ideas and/or themes, but is a dynamic involving memory and celebration of saving persons and events grounded in human experience and history. This is not to suggest that ideas or themes have no place in the celebrations of the liturgical year. For example, celebrations such as Trinity Sunday, and the Solemnity of the Body and Blood of Christ are rooted in refined theological ideas. Sometimes the actual history of a celebration reveals that it is rooted in an ideological concern. The genesis of the feast of St. Joseph the Worker (May 1), for example, was rooted in a reaction to communist May Day celebrations. At other times a celebration can become overly ideological by narrowing its focus too much. For example, when the espousal of virginity becomes the sole focus of the celebration of the memory of St. Maria Goretti, the feast can itself become both problematic and irrelevant because Maria Goretti was more than a virgin. Ideas and themes can and do have a place at times, but are generally a matter of secondary reflection.

The liturgical year is not simply a celebration of the various "life cycle events or rites of passage." The liturgical year has to do with the corporate memory and celebration of the whole ecclesial community. This is one reason why in many parishes infants are baptized in a fully community setting (sometimes at a particular Sunday eucharist). Life cycle events or rites of passage are situated within corporate memory and celebration. Here a proper understanding of the liturgical year suggests that all life cycle events and rites of passage have reference within the feasts and seasons of the year. For example, baptisms (outside of the paschal vigil), weddings and funerals ought to have reference to the cycle during which they are celebrated.

The liturgical year is not simply a celebration of time as an abstraction, nor is it a negotiable calculation of time. In the process of their development the feasts and seasons of the liturgical year paid close attention to cosmic elements. The experience of time was associated with solar and lunar movements, with light and darkness, with natural elements.

Some present celebrations of the liturgical year ignore these cosmic associations and this sometimes serves to impoverish liturgical celebrations. Some examples of this amnesia are: the celebration of vigils in the daylight, the celebration of evening prayer long before sunset, the simplistic importation of northern hemisphere cosmic elements into the southern hemisphere, the use of plastic, paper and silk flowers (especially outside their proper seasons).

The liturgical year is not necessarily in opposition to other celebrations of various yearly cycles. While Christian liturgy must be careful about admitting to its arena secular celebrations which bear distorted ideas, nevertheless, the authentically human in our society is the home of the good. What is needed here is a transformational approach to secular celebrations. Catholic Christians live and move in a broader society. We are neither sect nor cult. Celebrations which are good and pervasive in broader society are ignored in the liturgical arena at great risk. Thanksgiving and Independence Day, for example, are generally not ignored by Christians in their everyday lives. Should they simply be eclipsed in liturgy?

A LITURGICAL YEAR LIBRARY

The texts of the actual liturgical books themselves form the *primary texts* for the liturgical year. One cannot possibly hope to understand and appreciate the liturgical feasts and seasons without going directly to these liturgical books. The purpose of this present section is simply to name those liturgical books which are indispensable for celebrating and understanding the church's year.

Sacramentary. The *sacramentary* is used by the priest at mass. It contains a number of ritual instructions ("rubrics") as well as the presidential prayers (sometimes called "euchology") used at masses on Sundays and weekdays of Ordinary Time, Lent-Easter-Pentecost, Advent-Christmas-Epiphany, and the sanctoral cycle. In addition to these one will also find a number of texts for commons (for example, the common of the Blessed Virgin Mary), ritual masses (for example, the wedding mass), votive masses (for example, the Sacred Heart), masses for special needs (for example, for priestly vocations), masses for the dead, and appendices (for example, music for the order of mass). The *sacramentary* also contains the "General Instruction of the Roman Missal" as well as a number of other pertinent documents.

Lectionary. The *lectionary* contains the scriptural readings for use at liturgical celebrations. This book contains all the scripture readings for the various masses (mentioned above) as well as special "sequences" and verses for the gospel acclamation verses. Constant reference will be made in this work to the importance and structure of lectionary readings.

It has been customary in Christian liturgy to give the gospel a certain prominence. In a number of parishes a "Book of the Gospels" is used. This is a separate book containing the gospel lectionary readings. It is carried in the gospel procession by the deacon and it is from this book that the gospel is proclaimed.

Liturgy of the Hours. The *Liturgy of the Hours* is the church's official prayer for use throughout the various times of the day. In the comparatively recent past it had been the primary reserve of ordained ministers and members of some religious communities. The *Liturgy of the Hours* forms a sort of daily cycle of liturgical prayer. The *Liturgy of the Hours* will be discussed at greater length throughout this book. Here let it be noted that this liturgical prayer is a primary constituent of the theology and celebrations of the liturgical year.

General Norms for the Liturgical Year and Calendar. This is the English title for the official norms which govern the present liturgical year. Constant reference to these norms is made throughout this book. Familiarity with these norms is imperative for understanding and celebrating the liturgical year. In addition to the GNLYC, there exist a number of other Roman documents which ought to be consulted. Among these are the *Norms on Patron Saints* and the *Commentary on the General Norms for the Liturgical Year and Calendar.* The latter is a Roman commentary on the GNLYC.

The General Roman Calendar. This is the official list of solemnities, feasts, and memorials for use throughout the Roman Catholic Church. There also exist a *Commentary on the General Roman Calendar* as well as *The Proper Calendar for the Dioceses of the United States of America.* This proper calendar lists those celebrations which are particular to the United States. For example, some of the celebrations which are proper to the dioceses of the United States are:

January 4	St. Elizabeth Ann Seton (memorial)
January 5	St. John Neumann (memorial)
January 6	Blessed André Bessette (memorial)
March 3	Blessed Katherine Drexel (memorial)
May 15	St. Isidore (memorial)
July 4	Independence Day
July 14	Blessed Kateri Tekakwitha (memorial)
August 18	St. Jane Frances de Chantal (memorial)
September (first Monday)	Labor Day
September 9	St. Peter Claver (memorial)
October 6	Blessed Marie-Rose Durocher (memorial)
October 19	Sts. Isaac Jogues and John de Brébeuf and companions (memorial)
November 13	St. Frances Xavier Cabrini (memorial)
November 18	St. Rose Philippine Duchesne (memorial)
November (fourth Thursday)	Thanksgiving
December 12	Our Lady of Guadalupe (feast)

Religious orders and communities as well as individual dioceses may also have their own proper calendars.

Miscellaneous. In addition to the above texts there exist a number of other liturgical books which are helpful in unpacking the theology of the liturgical year.

The *Rite of Christian Initiation of Adults* must not be overlooked. This rite is very much connected to the Lent-Easter-Pentecost cycle and its euchology and lectionary texts are extremely important.

The recently published *Ceremonial of Bishops* is also a rich source of material. The *Ceremonial* contains a number of insightful theological and liturgical perspectives for the various feasts and seasons of the church's year. Part IV of the *Ceremonial,* "Celebrations of the Mysteries of the Lord through the Cycle of the Liturgical Year," is especially helpful.

One must not overlook the texts of other rites and rituals. Many of the various rites and rituals contain references to the liturgical year. For example, the *Book of Blessings* (which is part of *The Roman Ritual*) contains blessings for Advent wreaths, Christmas nativity scenes, Christmas trees, ashes (for Ash Wednesday), throats (on the Feast of St. Blaise), and so forth. The instructions and texts contained therein are quite helpful for understanding these various practices within the context of the liturgical year.

Hymnal. The liturgical year possesses its own special hymnal. The hymns and songs for the liturgical year can be found in the *Graduale Romanum* (*Roman Gradual*) and the *Liber Hymnarius* (*Book of Hymns*). The *Graduale Romanum* contains the song texts for use at the celebration of the eucharist. Texts are provided for the entrance, preparation of the gifts and communion. These are usually (though not always) taken from the scriptures. One can find the entrance and communion texts in the *sacramentary.* The *Liber Hymnarius* contains hymn texts for use during the Liturgy of the Hours. These texts should not be overlooked (though they often are) in understanding and celebrating the liturgical year.

A number of countries possess an official hymnal (for example, in Canada, the *Catholic Book of Worship*—the "officially approved hymnal for English-speaking Catholics in Canada"—is used). In the United States this is not the case. Thus, one would do well to have access to the major hymnals which are used in the United States. One would also do well to pay close attention to both the text and melody of liturgical songs because these are powerful conveyers of theology and spirit on a popular level. Among these hymnals presently published and used in parishes in the United States are:

Gather
Chicago: G.I.A. Publications, 1988.

Glory and Praise (in its various editions)
Phoenix: North American Liturgy Resources.

Hymnal for Catholic Students
Chicago: G.I.A. Publications, 1988.

Hymnal for the Hours (for use with the Liturgy of Hours)
Chicago: G.I.A. Publications, 1989.

Lead Me, Guide Me: The African American Catholic Hymnal
Chicago: G.I.A. Publications, 1987.

Peoples' Mass Book
Schiller Park: World Library Publications, 1984.

Worship (in its various editions and forms)
Chicago: G.I.A. Publications, 1986.

A GUIDE TO IMPORTANT LITURGICAL TEXTS

Having discussed the books which are basic to a working liturgical year library, the issue of specific liturgical texts can now be raised.

In the *sacramentary* the opening prayer, the prayer over the gifts, the prayer after communion, and the preface are particularly important for understanding the meaning of any given celebration. The opening prayer and preface (especially if a proper preface is provided) are indispensable. The prayer over the gifts and the prayer after communion generally tie the particular celebration to the general themes of those moments in the liturgy. It is in the opening prayer and the preface, however, that a particular theological perspective is given to the celebration. At times the "blessing over the people" (when one is provided) is also helpful.

In addition the entrance and communion antiphons should also be consulted (especially by those whose care it is to prepare the liturgical music).

These texts are generally referred to as the "proper" of the mass (in distinction from the "common" of the mass, that is, those texts which remain the same at each mass).

THE LITURGICAL YEAR—BASIC TEXTS

Sacramentary
opening prayer
prayer over gifts
prayer after communion

preface

blessing over people

entrance antiphon
communion antiphon

Lectionary
first reading
responsorial psalm
second reading
sequence?
gospel acclamation
gospel

Having consulted both the ***sacramentary*** and ***lectionary*** texts one might then raise a number of questions. Among these are: What theological and liturgical themes are present in the texts? What theological and liturgical images are present in the texts? What individual persons stand out in the texts? What is the liturgical theology of the feast or season which the text appears to propose? What is the context in which any given celebration is taking place? (For example, a funeral during the Advent-Christmas-Epiphany cycle might have a different tone than one which is celebrated during the Lent-Easter-Pentecost cycle.)

In addition to the mass texts the texts for the Liturgy of the Hours must not be overlooked (especially when "theologizing" about the liturgical year). These texts will be discussed in the next chapter.

For Personal Reflection and/or Group Discussion

1. Would you agree that all time is holy? Why or why not? Is some time holier than other time? What makes one time holier than other time? Could there be unholy or evil time?

2. Consult several **prefaces** from the various cycles and celebrations of the liturgical year. Where do you find evidence of an incarnational theology? Where do you find evidence of an eschatological approach to time?

3. Do you agree that liturgy often seems to lack a sense of the sacred and of mystery? What makes for a sense of the sacred and of mystery? If liturgy lacks it, how does one go about restoring it?

2

Pilgrim Liturgy for
a Pilgrim People

*Our liturgical ancestors clearly recognized that the way one
lived one's life was a litmus test of the authenticity of one's
worship. They knew in their bones that, in light of the insepara-
ble nature of liturgy and life, one must worship the same God
on Sunday and during the week, one must recognize that the
equality we know at the table of the Lord must be celebrated at
all our other tables; one must understand, perhaps daily more
deeply, the demands accepted with every liturgical Amen.*
KATHLEEN HUGHES, *VOICES OF THE EARLY
LITURGICAL MOVEMENT*

GENERAL HISTORICAL OVERVIEW

The liturgical year has not always been as elaborate, uniform or
well-structured as it is today. It developed gradually. Here only the
broadest sweeps of that development will be noted. The following
chapters will then deal in greater depth with each particular cycle as
well as individual major feasts within the given cycle.

The first Christian celebration to emerge was Sunday. It was
(and is) a weekly memorial of the Lord's death and resurrection.
During the second century an annual celebration of the Lord's paschal mystery also developed at Easter. Wednesdays and Fridays
were also given special attention. Christians fasted on these days and
then broke the fast around 3 p.m. with bread that remained from the
Sunday (possibly even a weekday) eucharist. This early period was
marked especially by a strong expectation of the glorious return of
Jesus (the ***parousia***).

There is evidence that during the third and fourth centuries an

23

annual celebration of the birth of Jesus became popular. Thus, by the fourth century, the weekly Sunday celebration, an annual celebration of the paschal mystery, and an annual commemoration of Jesus' birth were in place.

The emergence of celebrations in honor of martyrs and saints is difficult to trace. There appear to have been a number of annual feasts commemorating martyrs as early as the second century. It is possible, therefore, that such "sanctoral" celebrations (more precisely, "martyrial") were in place even before the commemoration of Christ's birth. What is certain is that these celebrations arose early and became quite popular both in terms of their number as well as the ceremonial with which they were surrounded.

During the Middle Ages a number of devotional or "idea" feasts also emerged. These were feasts that celebrated a particular devotion (for example, the cult of the blessed sacrament), or theological truth (for example, the feast of the Trinity), rather than an event in the life of Christ or some particular person.

By the Reformation era (ca. 1517 C.E.) the shape of the liturgical year as we know it in the west was in place. The times of Advent, Christmas, Lent and Easter were firmly established, and many of the feasts with which we are familiar were being celebrated. Unfortunately, the development of the calendar during the medieval and Reformation eras was problematic on several levels. The central place and significance of Sunday had been overshadowed by many other feasts. Christmas and its various celebrations (Advent, Epiphany, and so forth) eclipsed the place of Easter; the feasts in honor of the saints and Mary were overgrown, and popular devotions were far more important to people's spirituality than the liturgy.

These temptations toward overgrowth and reversals of priority have afflicted the calendar ever since. The recent reforms of the calendar which were initiated by Vatican II remind us that this continues to be the case.

JEWISH ROOTS OF THE LITURGICAL CALENDAR

Jesus was a Jew. The first Christian communities were Jewish in origin. Thus, the influence of Jewish teaching, law, customs and celebrations on the early shape of Christianity cannot be denied. It has become axiomatic to suggest that one cannot appreciate the Christian cycle of feasts and seasons unless one appreciates the Jewish festal calendar. With regard to the development of the liturgical year, however, balance and perspective are necessary. The study of the Jewish festal calendar is itself difficult because it borrowed much of its content and shape from surrounding peoples. There remains a great deal that is uncertain or unknown about the origins and development of the feasts of the Jewish calendar. As a matter of fact, the Hebrew scriptures reflect the influence of varying calendars, depending upon the period of authorship or the time of the events recounted. Thus, by the time of Jesus and the origins of the early Jesus movements within Judaism, the understanding of Jewish feasts had evolved.

Furthermore, one must remember that the development of the Christian year took place, for the most part, after the fall of Jerusalem. Much of the Christian liturgical year came into place after the expansion of Christianity among the Gentiles and in a Gentile context. In terms of origin and initial development, the Christian feasts and celebrations were greatly influenced by Judaism. However, with time, other forces also exerted influence on the shape and development of the liturgical year. Here we will simply note a few important factors in the Jewish influence on the liturgical year.

Characteristics. There are four general characteristics which should be remembered about the development of the Jewish festal calendar: 1) The oldest major feasts appear to have been pastoral and/or agricultural in nature. In time these feasts would have other meanings grafted onto them; 2) There were also familial feasts which were associated with the growth and maturation of persons; 3) There were certain **public** feasts which were political in nature (in a theocentric context), for example, the coronation of a king; 4) Finally, there also existed the possibility of including **lament** as a festal attitude. We tend to think of lamenting and feasting as being in opposition. However, the Israelite notion of feast had more to do with a *rendezvous,* a public gathering, than with a "let's be happy (however ungrounded)" attitude.

Nature. The Jewish calendar was influenced by the movements of both the sun and the moon. While the year as a whole was calculated by the sun, the position and the movement of the moon were also central, especially with regard to the calculation of feasts. The new moon and the full moon were of particular importance. Even today, in most Christian churches the lunar calendar influences the date of Easter.

Day. The Jewish notion of the "day" was sunset to sunset. Thus, feasts were generally celebrated from sunset to sunset. This notion has partly influenced the emergence of the rather recent practice of the Saturday evening mass. (This way of calculating the day was in contrast to the Greek notion of the day as dawn to dawn, and the Roman notion of the day as midnight to midnight.)

Sabbath. The origins of the Sabbath in the Jewish festal year remain unclear. Its existence dates back to the time of the Jewish exile (though it may have emerged earlier). It was a day given over to rest and worship.

The Jewish Sabbath has influenced the Christian Sunday in a number of respects. However, it has been the notion of the Sabbath as a day of rest which has exerted the most profound influence on the way in which Christians have traditionally celebrated Sunday. In its origins this rest was an ***imitatio Dei*** (imitation of God) who rested on the seventh day.

Pilgrimage Feasts. In addition to the Sabbath, the Jewish festal year consisted of a number of pilgrimage feasts. Every Jewish male twelve years of age and older was required to make a pilgrimage to Jerusalem each year for at least one of these feasts.

These feasts underwent transition throughout the history of the Jewish people. As these feasts developed many acquired new layers of meaning (and sometimes lost old layers of meaning). At the time of Jesus the pilgrimage feasts consisted of Passover, the Feast of Unleavened Bread, the Feast of Weeks, the Feast of Booths, the New Year feast, the Feast of Atonement, the Feast of the Dedication of the Temple and the Feast of Purim.

These feasts are of some significance to Christians because they are often the settings of narratives in the gospels and the Acts of the Apostles. Some have also been influential for the development of the theology of Christian feasts (for example, the Passover).

THE DEVELOPMENT OF THE LITURGICAL CALENDAR

The recent reforms of the liturgical calendar mandated by the Second Vatican Council stand with other such reforms in the church's history (most especially at the Council of Trent).

Prior To Trent. The shifts in the liturgical calendar prior to Trent reflect a movement from the simple to the complex. The various liturgical calendars in use from place to place were somewhat elaborate compared to the simplicity of the initial Christian liturgical calendar with its primary emphasis on the Lord's day.

Furthermore, it is impossible to speak about a uniform Roman calendar as such. The many and various sacramentaries and lectionaries from the period between 600 C.E. and 1500 C.E. reveal that different geographical regions possessed their own unique liturgical calendars. This does not mean that common feasts did not exist. Rather, it eliminates the notion that a uniform Roman calendar existed. One must speak about many calendars rather than one calendar.

Unfortunately a number of questionable practices arose. For example, the number of saints celebrated in the sanctoral cycle increased to the detriment of the more central theological and liturgical dynamisms of the calendar, particularly the paschal mystery. Thus, the sanctoral feasts came to overshadow the central place of Sunday and to disrupt the integrity of the liturgical seasons. Certain liturgical abuses (for example, multiple masses for the dead) as well as quasi-superstitious practices also weakened the central theological and liturgical dynamisms.

Immediately prior to the Reformation, therefore, there was need for reform of the calendar. The number of saints' feasts was excessive. In many places votive masses for the dead were celebrated as the norm rather than the exception. The centrality of Sunday was usurped by feasts such as those in honor of the Trinity and the blessed sacrament (which continue to be celebrated on Sunday in the United States). Cluttered by votive masses and sanctoral celebrations, liturgical seasons lost their theological significance. Furthermore, extra-liturgical practices (such as rosaries, novenas and indulgences) tended to be far more crucial in the life of the ordinary Christian than was the liturgy itself. Against this backdrop both Pius V (1566–1572) and Gregory XIII (1572–1585) undertook a reform of the calendar.

Trent and Its Reforms. Before proceeding to the actual reforms two important factors must be noted: 1) The calendar reforms of Pope Gregory XIII must be seen in relation to the earlier reforms of the Roman Missal (1570) and the Roman Breviary (1568); 2) The reform of the calendar at this point involved an astronomical as well as a liturgical reform. At this time the calendar of Julius Caesar which had been in use needed modification. Miscalculations regarding the actual length of the solar revolution had led to a shifting in the actual day of the spring equinox. By the sixteenth century the reform of this calendar necessitated the suppression of ten days of the calendar. On February 24, 1582, a Bull was issued by Pope Gregory XIII which mandated such a suppression.

Regarding the liturgical year, the following reforms emerged. First, there was a reduction in the number of sanctoral celebrations from roughly 300 to 150. Along with the enumeration of feasts there was also a clarification concerning their rank in importance. Interestingly enough these same kinds of reform were also mandated by the Second Vatican Council.

Another reform which emerged was the relative centralization and uniformity of the liturgical calendar. The printing press was pivotal in assuring the success of this centralization and uniformity.

Over time these reforms were augmented by others. For example, in 1602 Clement VIII added another rank of importance to the already existing five ranks. This served to complicate the calendar. The subsequent centuries also saw a new explosion of sanctoral, and especially marian, celebrations. For example, during this period the following marian celebrations were added: Holy Name of Mary (1683), Our Lady of Ransom (1696), Our Lady of the Rosary (1716), Our Lady of Mount Carmel (1726), Compassion of Mary (1727), Seven Sorrows of the Blessed Virgin Mary (1814), Our Lady of Lourdes (1907), Motherhood of Mary (1931), Immaculate Heart of Mary (1942), and the Queenship of Mary (1954). The number of sanctoral celebrations increased from 149 to 280 during this period.

One gets the picture. By the 1960s the liturgical year was once again overgrown and was ripe for reform.

Vatican II. The recent reforms of the Roman Catholic calendar were initiated by the Second Vatican Council. However, these reforms did not emerge from a vacuum. One can speak about "phases" when discussing these reforms.

Phase one was actually the liturgical movement which took place prior to the Second Vatican Council. Today names such as Lambert Beauduin (1873–1960), Romano Guardini (1885–1968), and Virgil Michel (1890–1938) are associated with this movement. However, there also emerged a number of official liturgical reforms from the highest ecclesial authorities. For example, Pope Pius X initiated a revision which restricted the number of feasts which could be celebrated on a Sunday. Pope Pius XII was responsible for the initial revisions of the paschal triduum which took place in the 1950s.

The second phase came to focus in the Vatican II's "Constitution on the Sacred Liturgy" (promulgated December 4, 1963) (hereafter CSL). Chapter 5 specifically addressed the reforms of the liturgical year which were to be undertaken. Chapter 5 may be divided into two parts. The first part (#102–105) establishes the theological foundations of the liturgical year. Among these foundations are:

> **#102.** The centrality of keeping the memory of the passion and resurrection of Christ is noted. This is done in the weekly Sunday celebration as well as the annual celebration of Easter. This memory is also kept in all the celebrations of the liturgical year, from the celebration of the incarnation to the celebration of Pentecost, and the Lord's expected return.

> **#103.** Mary, who is inseparably bound to the work of her son, Jesus Christ, is also honored.

> **#104.** The church also remembers the martyrs and other saints in annual cycle days. They were perfected by the grace of God and are now in possession of eternal life. In

this state they sing the praise of God and offer prayers for those on earth. Furthermore, they are models of sanctity to the whole Christian community.

#105. Pious practices, instruction, prayer, and works of penance and mercy are also dimensions of the liturgical year.

The subsequent six paragraphs of the constitution then address specific reforms which emerge from these foundational observations.

#106. The restoration of the importance of Sunday celebrations is recognized. Hence, other celebrations, unless truly of overriding importance, must not eclipse Sunday which is the heart of the liturgical year.

#107. The importance of seasonal celebrations is to be restored. These seasonal celebrations should reflect the centrality of the paschal mystery.

#108. The importance of the mysteries of salvation as these are celebrated through the feasts of the Lord should be restored. Because of this the season of the "Proper of Time" (which we now call Ordinary Time) is to be given prominence. Feasts in honor of the saints should not eclipse feasts of the Lord.

#109. Proper attention should be given Lent as both a baptismal and penitential period.

#110. A proper understanding of lenten penance as both social and external (as well as private and internal) should be restored.

#111. The saints have traditionally been honored because their lives of holiness reflect Christ and encourage the faithful. However, only those saints who are truly significant for the whole church should be celebrated in the universal calendar. Other sanctoral celebrations should be shifted to the calendars of dioceses and/or religious communities.

These paragraphs became the charter for the reform of the liturgical year which emerged after the Vatican Council. We are now living in this third phase. During this time there have emerged the reformed general Roman calendar, the ***General Norms for the Liturgical Year and the Calendar,*** the "Commentary" on the ***General Norms,*** the ***lectionary,*** the ***sacramentary,*** and a number of other documents and books. (See "A Liturgical Year Library" discussed in chapter 1.)

THE LITURGY OF THE HOURS: A DAILY CYCLE

The Liturgy of the Hours will be considered in each chapter vis-à-vis its relationship to the seasonal cycle under discussion. The purpose of this present section is to provide a historical, theological and liturgical base for the importance of this often overlooked liturgy.

History. At the time of Jesus the daily synagogue liturgy evidently consisted of three services: a morning service, an afternoon service, and an evening service. The primary reason for these services was "covenant-mindfulness"—to preserve the memory of the covenant. The early Jewish Christian communities probably continued to attend these services until a break occurred between Judaism and Christianity ca. 135 C.E.

Once the split occurred, the Christians continued to pray three times daily, but within a familial (household) context that this happened. Their prayer had certain eschatological overtones. They "watched and prayed" for Jesus' return.

During the second and third centuries it appears that prayer at dawn and twilight was obligatory for most Christians. They were also exhorted to pray at other times of the day (for example, the third, sixth and ninth hours). Certain themes began to be associated with the dawn and twilight prayer. Morning prayer became associated with the resurrection, and twilight prayer became associated with Jesus' passion and burial.

During the fourth to sixth centuries two styles of daily prayer emerged. The cathedral style (sometimes referred to as "parochial" or "ecclesiastical") was a *popular* style marked by symbols and ceremonies (for example, light, incense and processions), easily remembered chants (for example, responsories and antiphons), a diversity of ministerial functions (for example, deacons, readers, psalmists), and by a choice of psalmody that was limited and select. The monastic style was marked by greater ceremonial and symbolic restraint, was often longer, and involved continuous psalmody. In time, as church leaders were chosen from among the monks, the influence of the monastic style of prayer dominated.

With the rise of the mendicant communities (who were "on the go"—the Franciscans and Dominicans) there was a need for one book which could travel easily. Thus, the "breviary" appeared. The Franciscans eventually adopted the "Office" used at the papal chapel, and as they spread throughout Europe so did this particular Office.

As a result of the Council of Trent, the official daily prayer was revised, and in 1568 the *Roman Breviary* was published. This was modified a number of times until Vatican II.

The Second Vatican Council mandated the revision of the *Liturgy of the Hours.* As a result, the *General Instruction of the Liturgy of the Hours* (hereafter GILH) appeared on February 2, 1971. During 1970–1971 the Latin edition appeared, and during 1974 an English edition was made available in the United States.

In many respects this revised daily liturgical prayer was a great advance over the former *Roman Breviary.* It is, however, not without its shortcomings. Among these are: 1) The commission who prepared it was primarily concerned with producing a prayer book for the clergy and members of religious orders. Unfortunately the parish/parochial context was eclipsed. 2) It seems to have been the presumption that this prayer would be prayed privately rather than in common. 3) The source for the revision seems to have been dominated by a postmedieval Latin tradition. A closer look at earlier premedieval traditions might have helped.

It is this most recent revision that is presently used by the clergy, many religious communities, and some parishes (with modifications). To its theological and liturgical principles we now turn our attention.

Liturgy. The Liturgy of the Hours is, first of all, liturgy. This might appear as a ridiculously simple statement, but it must continually be emphasized. This liturgy continues to be overlooked in many parishes and communities.

The Liturgy of the Hours is rooted in, and is the outgrowth of our tradition of liturgical prayer. It is one of the gifts of our liturgical tradition. The Liturgy of the Hours by its nature as liturgy is both public (as opposed to private) and common (as opposed to being proper simply to *me*). This, however, is not to suggest that the Liturgy of the Hours cannot and/or should never be prayed by an individual apart from a gathered community.

Sanctification of Time. The Liturgy of the Hours involves the sanctification of time. The GILH states that: "The purpose of the Liturgy of the Hours is to sanctify the day and the whole range of human activity" (#11). This is not to suggest that all other time is unholy (or, for that matter, holy). Rather, even time itself must be brought under the scrutiny of gospel values.

Within the context of the Liturgy of the Hours time itself is related to the whole of the cosmos. For that reason the individual hours (with the exception of the "Office of Readings") are attuned to cosmic dynamics. For example, many of the texts of morning prayer are attuned to dawn, just as many of the texts and ritual actions of evening prayer are attuned to dusk.

The Liturgy of the Hours in its entirety consists of the following:

1. *Office of Readings:* This differs from the other hours in that it is not related to a particular time of the day and its focus is more heavily "reading" (usually one passage from the scriptures and one from a church document or one of the church fathers).

2. *Morning Prayer*

3. *Midmorning Prayer*

4. *Midday Prayer*

5. *Midafternoon Prayer*

6. *Evening Prayer*

7. *Night Prayer:* This hour is to be prayer immediately before retiring for bed.

This relationship is one of the dimensions of the Liturgy of the Hours that distinguishes it from many other liturgical celebrations. It is distributed throughout the entire day and it is intricately related to particular moments and cosmic movements. Ironically enough, an eclipse of this relationship to the natural rhythms of day and night continues to haunt many celebrations of the Liturgy of the Hours.

One sometimes hears it said that the Liturgy of the Hours concerns the sanctification of time, whereas the eucharistic liturgy has to do with eschatological praying (that is, praying related to the final coming of Christ). However, care must be taken lest a false dichotomy be established between the relationship of time to the eucharist and the hours. All liturgy is by its nature eschatological. The Liturgy of the Hours involves the sanctification of time as well as eschatological praying. The very doing of liturgy and sacrament on this side of death is a reminder that we are still waiting. Though there are moments of supreme and dense disclosure, the eschatological pull of liturgy remains. Liturgy is never simply cultic self-preoccupation.

Praise and Petition. "The Liturgy of the Hours or Divine Office, enriched by readings, is principally a prayer of praise and petition" (GILH #2). It is important to note the "praise and petition" nature of the Liturgy of the Hours. Though it is certainly rooted in the sacred scriptures, the Liturgy of the Hours is not primarily a proclamation of the word.

Structure of the Hinge Hours. The GILH speaks about morning and evening prayer as the "hinge" hours, that is, the most important hours of the day. The structure of these hours follows the same pattern.

1. Invitation to Prayer.

2. Hymn: "The purpose of the hymn is to set the tone for the hour or the feast and, especially in celebration with a congregation, to form a simple and pleasant introduction to prayer" (GILH #42).

3. Psalmody: Psalmody here includes both the psalms and canticles from the Hebrew and Christian scriptures. In the morning the pattern is: psalm, Hebrew canticle, psalm. The theme of the first psalm is generally related to the morning. The second psalm is usually a psalm of praise.

   In the evening the pattern is: psalm, psalm, canticle from the Christian scriptures. Some of the psalms have been chosen in terms of the evening hour, for example, Psalm 141.

   The psalms are sometimes followed by "psalm prayers" which help us to understand the psalms from a Christian perspective.

4. Reading.

5. Response: This may be eliminated in favor of silence.

6. Gospel canticle: In the morning the Canticle of Zechariah is prayed. In the evening the Canticle of Mary is prayed.

7. Invocations/Intercessions.

8. The Lord's Prayer.

9. The collect.

10. The blessing/dismissal.

Texts. The Liturgy of the Hours also contains texts which are proper, that is, they vary according to season and/or feast. These proper texts are a rich source for developing a liturgical theology of any given feast or season.

Chief among these is the *hymn.* In the west the text hymn developed as a genre that was particularly suited to the Liturgy of the

Hours. It was (and is) a rich source for understanding the liturgical theology of a feast. These hymns should not be neglected. Also to be noted are: proper antiphons, readings, responses, intercessions/petitions, and collects.

GENERAL PASTORAL ISSUES

In each subsequent chapter pastoral issues specific to each of the cycles will be discussed. Here, however, a few general foundational issues need consideration.

Customs and Secular Celebrations. Some dialectic ought to be maintained between liturgical cycles/feasts and popular extraliturgical customs associated with cultural celebrations. A great deal of prudence, however, is needed in this area. There are a number of secular and cultural celebrations which may have no place in Christian liturgy and/or spirituality. The church, however, has tended to look kindly on cultural and ethnic celebrations and, where possible, has sought to "baptize" them. Oddly enough, there appears to be a growing tendency today simply to dismiss such celebrations as inappropriate to the arena of liturgy. This can lead to a growing schizophrenia in the Christian community.

Any number of examples illustrate this point. The celebration of the feast of Mary, Mother of God on New Year's Day (in the west) is one example. While liturgical texts exist for such a New Year's Day celebration in the **sacramentary** these cannot be used because the Mary, Mother of God celebration is a solemnity. The complete eclipse of St. Valentine's Day in the liturgical arena is another example.

The Arts. In the cycles and celebrations of the liturgical year both music and environment are themselves interpretive acts. For this reason art and environment are never secondary. They are always primary acts of interpretation. They often create an affective (and effective) opening into the meaning of a cycle or celebration. This affective opening is sometimes more powerful than the liturgical texts themselves. There are times when these "con-texts" actually overwhelm the "texts" and assume the major role in arbitrating the meaning of feasts and seasons. Simply recollecting the role of the crèche at Christmas suffices to illustrate this point. For this reason music and environment must be carefully attended to.

WOMEN'S MEMORIES AND THE LITURGICAL YEAR

Recent United Nations statistics reveal that while women comprise fifty percent of the world's population, they do seventy-five percent of the world's work and receive ten percent of the world's salary. This sad and unjust statistic is also at times reflected in the Catholic church, especially in the celebrations of the liturgical year. Women are largely absent from the lectionary and when they do appear it is often either as adjuncts to men, or in a negative context. For example, the woman of John 8, the woman "caught in adultery," appears in the lectionary while quite a number of exemplary women from both the Hebrew and Christian scriptures have simply been eclipsed. Even when women do appear in a positive light, a homily is often given from a patriarchal and/or androcentric perspective. For example, how many people realize that Mary Magdalene and other women were actually the first witnesses to the resurrection, as well as the first to bear testimony to the risen Jesus?

The presence of women in the sanctoral cycle holds out hope, but here there are problems as well. The present sanctoral cycle remains too male-dominated. For example, the men far outnumber the women. In the universal calendar there are forty-five obligatory memorials of men while there are only thirteen obligatory memorials of women. Likewise there are sixty-five optional memorials of men while there are only ten of women. The real impact and relevance of these optional memorials is questionable. Remember they are *optional,* and when used, their prayers tend to be less filled out. The names and memories of these women of the optional memorials may, therefore, be further eclipsed in the liturgical assembly. The calendar for the United States is helpful in that it adds a few more women.

A further problem may be the primary prism through which the women are viewed, that is, as "virgin." This is not to denigrate virginity, but when it becomes the exclusive or primary image through which holy women are viewed it can become problematic.

It can especially limit our appreciation for individual persons as persons. For example, Maria Goretti sometimes becomes a whipping post to address teenage (and adult) sexual license. However, there are other possibilities here. Maria Goretti could serve to highlight the situation of those who have been unjustly victimized, as well as the dangers of an elite "adultism." She could illustrate that children and teenagers are capable of holiness precisely as children and teenagers. The fact that there are so few married women saints in the calendar may be indicative of the problem encountered when "virgin" becomes one of the few images by which to celebrate women's holiness. In light of this a special word is in order regarding women's memories, the liturgical year, and pastoral liturgical strategies. Among these liturgical strategies are:

1. Capitalize on the women who are mentioned in the lectionary texts. A *feminist anamnesis* is necessary here. Consciously attempt to view and understand these women from a less patriarchal and androcentric perspective. For example, capitalize on Mary Magdalene and the other women as the first witnesses of the risen Jesus. Capitalize on Mary (sister of Martha and Lazarus) and her profession of faith ("You are the Christ"), which is similar to Peter's. We need to take the presence and witness of these women seriously.

Here one might entertain the celebration of seasonal services which consciously seek to move biblical and sanctoral cycle women center-stage. For example, during Advent a service might highlight women's stories using Matthew's genealogy and the four women who appear therein.

2. Take advantage of the possibilities for celebrating the memory of the women saints in the sanctoral cycle. Do not be afraid to celebrate the optional memorials. For example, Rose of Lima (August 23) is an optional memorial, yet she was the first canonized saint of the New World. Furthermore, in her care for children and the elderly she helped established some of the initial forms of social outreach to others in the New World. Do not be afraid to tell the whole story even when that story involves conflict with church and/or state. Sometimes this story is eclipsed through distortion, misrepresentation or reinterpretation. Also, be careful about the image through which one views the saints (women or men). There are other possibilities besides virgin.

3. Be attentive to the place of women in the visual arts, especially in items such as worship leaflets. These often continue to be dominated by male images. Also, be careful *how* women are imaged in the arts.

4. Be consciously attentive to the role and place of women in all the celebrations of the liturgical year. Women should be both visible and audible as ministers in the liturgy.

For Personal Reflection and/or Group Discussion

1. If you were a member of another religious tradition observing Christians celebrating their liturgical seasons and feasts, which Christ season and/or feast would strike you as most important? Why? Which would strike you as least important? Why?

2. At this point in your reading, which Christian feast do you consider to be theologically and liturgically most central? Why?

3. Why is it necessary to understand the origins of the Jewish feasts in order to appreciate some of the feasts of the Christian liturgical year?

4. Do you agree that too many sanctoral and marian celebrations can clutter the liturgical calendar? Why or why not?

5. Can you think of present customs and practices in the Catholic community which are the result of a "baptism" of culture? What present customs and celebrations in North American culture might be "baptized" by the Catholic community?

6. Do you agree that the stories and memories of women have often been eclipsed in the liturgy? Why or why not? Do you agree that a more concerted effort is needed to keep women's memories alive in the liturgy? Why or why not?

3

Sunday and Ordinary Time

. . . the liturgy does not passively await an absent eschaton. It celebrates the eschaton's unfolding presence every Sunday, the Lord's resurrection day. For this reason, there is no such thing as "ordinary time" in Christian worship. Nor is Sunday a little Easter; Easter is a big Sunday, that one Sunday of the fifty-two which follows the day of Christ's work on the cross and his sabbath rest in the tomb.

AIDAN KAVANAGH, *ELEMENTS OF RITE*

To this last supper he has summoned them,
and (like a shot that scatters birds from trees)
their hands draw back from reaching for the loaves
upon his word: they fly across to him;
they flutter, frightened, round the supper
table searching for an escape. But he is present
everywhere like an all-pervading twilight-hour.

RAINER MARIA RILKE,
ON SEEING LEONARDO DA VINCI'S 'LAST SUPPER', MILAN 1904

HISTORICAL BACKGROUND

Sundays. Tracing the development of Sunday is no easy task. The history of its development is complex and there are a number of gaps which as yet remain purely hypothetical. This brief historical overview will attempt to present some general information which is commonly held among scholars as well as some interesting hypothetical information which might be helpful.

The early Jewish Christian communities evidently continued to gather in their synagogues for the celebration of the Sabbath. These synagogue gatherings were much like a "liturgy of the word." The scriptures were proclaimed and explained. At this early stage the Christian identity was one which was still thoroughly tied to Jewish practices. In addition to the Sabbath assemblies the Jewish Christians would also gather for the "breaking of the bread." It is difficult to say with any certainty on what days and how often they gathered for this breaking of the bread. The question remains whether a spirituality and theology of Sunday as a special day gave rise to a Sunday eucharist or the eucharistic gathering gave rise to Sunday as a special day. Was Sunday important as a day in itself, or was it important because it was the day on which the eucharist was celebrated? Much has to do with how one interprets the meaning of the breaking of the bread (e.g., Acts 2:42) and the eucharist. These terms may not necessarily be synonymous and one must be extremely careful about reading later liturgical and theological interpretations into these gatherings. The celebration of what we would call the eucharist evidently took place within the context of a fuller meal called an *agape.* Even that distinction, however, may be anachronistic.

What can be stated with some certainty is that a number of factors contributed to an eventual change in the worship patterns of the early Jewish Christians. Among these are: the fall of Jerusalem, a growing antagonism between Jewish Christians and other Jews, the admittance of Gentiles to the church (without requiring certain Jewish practices) and the general spread of the Christian message.

Current historical evidence suggests that in and around Rome in the second century, Sunday was the day of Christian assembly. However, it must again be noted that there may have been varying practices according to place and time. The reasons for this shift to Sunday were many—some religious, some political, some ideological. Among these were: the first day of the week as the day of resurrection; the post-resurrection appearances of Jesus on the first day of the week; the image of the first day as also the "eighth day" with its notions of creation and re-creation; the problem with the cult associated with the sun god; the emperor Trajan's edict in which clubs of friends (with their common meals) were outlawed; and a possible (probable?) subtle anti-Judaism. Of particular importance was Trajan's edict, for it seems that at that point the eucharist became separated from the *agape.* The eucharist began to be celebrated during the early morning hours.

The question of the Sunday rest did not factor in at this point. This first day of the week was simply another workday. Thus, many of the Christians actually worked on Sunday and met after work for the Sunday eucharistic celebration. After Trajan's edict, of course, they met in the morning.

By the fourth century Sunday became the day for Christians to assemble for worship throughout most of the Roman Empire. With the eventual alignment of church and state Sunday became a day of rest. In 321 C.E. Constantine issued an edict which officially recognized Sunday as a day of rest. This marked an important shift because it grafted a new layer of meaning onto Sunday, that is, Sunday as a day of rest, an image which survives to this day.

This weekly assembly of Christians preceded any annual liturgical celebrations. It was only later that various Christian communities came to celebrate feasts such as Christmas, Easter, Pentecost, martyrs' days, and so forth. Thus, chronologically speaking, the Sunday celebration takes a certain priority over other celebrations.

The early Christians understood their Sunday celebrations through the prism of varying analogues. One particularly important analogue was "the Lord's day." This title was probably derived from one of the common names for the eucharist, "the Lord's supper." It therefore tends to underscore the relationship between Sunday and the celebration of the eucharist. Another important analogue is the "eighth day," which was partially a metaphor implying the notion of re-creation. The re-creation of humanity and cosmos was accomplished in the resurrection which was celebrated in the Sunday eucharistic gathering. The eighth day is likewise associated with the end times.

The meaning of the Sunday celebration was eventually eclipsed. By the time of the Reformation and the Council of Trent, the centrality of Sunday as the celebration of the Lord's day was overshadowed by feasts such as those in honor of the Trinity and the blessed sacrament. It was this context which served as a backdrop for the reforms of the calendar that were undertaken by Pius V (1566–1572) and Gregory XIII (1572–1585). Part of this reforming dynamic was a concern to restore the importance of the meaning of Sunday in itself (rather than in relationship to some other feast).

The Second Vatican Council in its "Constitution on the Sacred Liturgy" sought once again to highlight the importance of Sunday (see para. #106). With regard to the celebration of other liturgical feasts on Sunday the council noted that "other celebrations, unless they be truly of overriding importance, must not have precedence over this day, which is the foundation and nucleus of the whole liturgical year" (para. #106). The GNLYC continued this notion by stating that "Sunday must be ranked as the first holy day of all" (para. #4).

The Sunday Obligation. The notion of Sunday as a day of obligatory presence at worship reaches back to the Council of Elvira in 306 C.E. It decreed that "if anyone in the city does not attend church three Sundays, let him or her abstain (from receiving the eucharist) in order that he or she may be seen to be rebuked." The **meaning** of this canon, however, is disputed because of its somewhat ambiguous language. There are two questions which have been raised. First, the nature of the obligation in question has been disputed. Was the obligation simply to worship, or was it rather, the deeper and fuller obligation to participate in the whole life of the church? Indeed, can the two really be separated? Second, the actual subject of the obligation has been disputed. Was the council speaking about a collective obligation (due to the absence of large numbers from Sunday eucharist) which would apply more fully to the church in general, or was the notion of obligation simply aimed at individual Christians? The point here is that one must interpret the canon carefully. It was not until the Council of Aged in 506 C.E. that there is an undisputed and explicitly stated obligation to attend Sunday mass.

Canon 1247 of the present *Code of Canon Law* states that "on Sundays and other holy days of obligation the faithful are bound to participate in the Mass. . . ." This same canon also states that the faithful should "abstain from those labors and business concerns which impede the worship to be rendered to God. . . ." If participation in the eucharist is impossible because of a lack of a "sacred minister" then participation in a liturgy of the word "in the parish church or in another sacred place according to the prescriptions of the diocesan bishop" is recommended (Canon 1248). If this is not available then engagement in prayer for "an appropriate amount of time personally or in a family or, as occasion offers, in groups of families" is recommended (Canon 1248).

Weekdays. In time the various weekdays also developed liturgically. This happened differently from place to place. For example, early in the history of some communities Wednesdays and Fridays developed as fast days. Furthermore, in some places Saturday became a liturgical day (associated with the Jewish Sabbath), while in other places it became a strictly a-liturgical day.

With the ongoing development of Christian theology and the emergence of certain devotional patterns, the various weekdays developed their own devotional-liturgical overtones. From Trent on, specific days were associated with particular votive celebrations. Monday came to be dedicated to the Trinity; Tuesday, to the angels (including the guardian angels); Wednesday, to the apostles (also, from 1920 on to St. Joseph or Sts. Peter and Paul); Thursday, to the Holy Spirit (also, from 1604 on to the holy eucharist, and from 1935 on to the priesthood of Christ); Friday, to the cross, the passion of Christ, the sacred heart of Jesus, or the precious blood; and Saturday, to Mary. Many of these are still known to contemporary Catholic Christians. For example, it remains customary in many places to associate Saturday with Mary and to honor her by using the liturgical texts of one of the votive masses of Mary.

Ordinary Time. Prior to the recent reform of the liturgical year, "Ordinary Time" as a liturgical term did not exist. In the previous calendar there was time "after Epiphany" and time "after Pentecost." The length of these seasons could vary depending on the data of Easter.

In the 1969 reforms, the designation of time "after Epiphany" and "after Pentecost" disappeared, and there emerged the notion of "Ordinary Time" in the liturgical year. The reason for this change is twofold. First, the former titles tended to link these Sundays with the feast named (that is, Epiphany and Pentecost), with the overall liturgical cycle in which they occurred. Thus, Epiphany became divorced from Advent-Christmas and Pentecost became divorced from Lent-Easter. Furthermore, their unique Sunday nature was obscured. Second, the former designation tended to eclipse the fundamental unity of the time "after Epiphany" and "after Easter." The common title, Ordinary Time, seeks to restore a sense of this unity. This Ordinary Time consists of 33 to 34 weeks. These Sundays are not associated with any particular feast; thus, the time is not counted "after Epiphany" or "after Pentecost." The Sundays that occur during this time possess their own unique liturgical character which is reflected in their proper prayers and scriptural texts. The GNLYC notes that the weeks of this period, especially in the Sunday celebrations "are devoted to the mystery of Christ in all its aspects" (para. #43). The weekdays of Ordinary Time also have their own proper lectionary texts.

Ordinary Time begins on Monday after the Sunday following January 6 (in the United States that Sunday is usually the feast of the Baptism of the Lord) and continues until the Tuesday before Ash Wednesday. It picks up again on the Monday after Pentecost Sunday and ends before evening prayer I of the First Sunday of Advent (GNLYC #44).

The Liturgical Day. There have been and continue to be different ways of calculating and marking the transition of daily time. With regard to the liturgical day the GNLYC notes that normally it "runs from midnight to midnight, but the observance of Sunday and solemnities begins with the evening of the preceding day" (para. #3). This same article also notes that: "Each day is made holy through the liturgical celebrations of the people of God, especially through the eucharistic sacrifice and the divine office" (that is, the Liturgy of the Hours).

GENERAL PRINCIPLES

Ordinary? There is nothing "ordinary" about Sunday. Generally speaking, Sunday never takes a holiday. It must be remembered that Sundays are celebrated during both "ordinary time" and the various seasonal cycles. While attention must always be given to the particular seasonal cycle during which a Sunday is celebrated, the Sunday celebrations of liturgical seasons still participate in the various analogues by which all Sundays are understood (for example, the eighth day image, the Lord's day, the day of the Lord's resurrection, and so forth).

The GNLYC (para. #6) notes that other celebrations are not to be assigned to Sunday, with the following exceptions: the feasts of the Holy Family and the Baptism of the Lord, and the solemnities of the Holy Trinity and Christ the King. In places where Epiphany, Ascension, and Corpus Christi are not celebrated as holy days of obligation, these celebrations are also transferred to Sunday. Again, this is not to suggest that the usual Sunday analogues are suspended. The various Sunday analogues must interact dialectically with these feasts and solemnities. The celebration of these various feasts and solemnities ought not eclipse the Sunday celebration such that its "Sunday" flavor is lost. (However, one must be careful about overloading certain Sundays, or any day, with too many meanings.)

The GNLYC also notes that feasts and solemnities should never take precedence over the Sundays of Advent, Lent, and Easter (para. #5). There is a certain internal coherence to the Sundays of these times which should not be broken. This internal coherence will become more evident in the chapters which follow.

There is also a certain coherence about the various Sundays of Ordinary Time. Care must be taken not to allow these Sundays to slip through the cracks. There is a tendency in some parishes and communities to spend much time and energy preparing for the Sundays which occur within the framework of liturgical seasons (for example, Advent-Christmas-Epiphany and Lent-Easter-Pentecost), while taking a rest from any involved preparation during the Sunday celebrations of Ordinary Time. Yet there is nothing ordinary about either Ordinary Time or its Sundays. It might be more helpful to speak about "Sundays of the Year." The use of the word "ordinary" is somewhat confusing here. Ordinary Time is not simply "time in between," nor is it "ordinary" in contrast to "extraordinary." From a Christian perspective there is no time which is ordinary. What is at issue here is not so much a *quality* of time, but rather, a *quantity* of time in terms of enumerating and designating. The notion of "ordinary" here is related to *ordinal* numbers, as in the process of counting. Thus, the reformed calendar speaks of the

"Second Sunday of Ordinary Time," and so forth. Perhaps it might be helpful to understand and image Ordinary Time as itself a season —the *longest* season of the church's liturgical year. One might make a case for understanding and celebrating Ordinary Time as the most significant of the liturgical seasons precisely because of its length. It is a season of "diaphony" in which the church becomes more deeply aware of the presence of God within the ordinary. It is this Ordinary Time of the liturgical year which is celebrated throughout the course of an individual's and a community's ordinary times of the year.

Weekly Easter? Every Sunday is a "weekly Easter" and more besides. It has become customary in some circles to refer to Sunday as a "weekly Easter" (or "little Easter"). There is certainly truth to this notion, but it is a partial truth. A "weekly Easter" is but one analogue by which Sunday can be understood. Others have been mentioned above.

Theologically and liturgically speaking, Sunday is a celebration of the paschal mystery, of which the mystery of Easter is but a part. Furthermore, to refer to Sunday as a "weekly Easter" is to run the risk of collapsing the differences between the weekly celebration of Sunday and the annual celebration of Easter. A more adequate image might be Sunday as a "weekly triduum" having at its heart the paschal mystery, of which the life, passion and death of the Lord are also dimensions. Sunday can also be said to be a "weekly Pentecost" celebrating as it does certain eschatological overtones which are captured by the images of the "eighth day" and the "day of rest." The Lord, after all, sent the Holy Spirit on his disciples on the first day of the week.

Those paschal overtones are beautifully enunciated in a number of the Sunday prefaces. For example, in the first preface for Sundays in Ordinary Time we pray: "Through his [Christ's] cross and resurrection he freed us from sin and death and called us to the glory. . . ." Again, in the fourth preface we pray: "In his suffering we are freed from sin. By his rising from the dead we rise to everlasting life. In his return to you in glory we enter into your heavenly kingdom."

Foundation. Sunday is at the heart and foundation of the liturgical year. The Christian community gathers on Sunday each week, fifty-two times a year. That Sunday is at the heart of the liturgical year should hardly be surprising as the historical evidence clearly suggests that the Sunday celebration preceded chronologically the Easter celebration.

Entirety. The entire Sunday is celebrated. Christian communities have a tendency to reduce the celebration of Sunday to a fifty-five minute eucharist. The celebration of Sunday, however, is more than simply the celebration of the eucharist. This is hardly a plea for longer eucharists. It is, however, a recognition of and plea for greater possibilities for the gathering of Christians on Sunday, both liturgically and socially. Sunday is, after all, the day for Christian assembly. Perhaps possibilities for family recreation, special table prayers, parish picnics and Sunday evening prayer might serve nicely to fill out Sunday.

One must be careful, however, in justifying this observation. The Christian Sunday should not simply be thought of as the Jewish "Sabbath" with Christian layers of meaning grafted onto it. The Christian Sunday is different. For example, the notion of Sabbath rest is inextricably bound to the Jewish celebration of Sabbath. This is neither historically nor theologically the case with Sunday. Remember that Sunday was originally a workday. What evidently gave Sunday its unique character was the celebration of the eucharist, not rest from work.

Eucharist. The celebration of the eucharist is especially proper to Sunday. There is a question of ecclesiology which is embedded here. The church makes the eucharist makes the church makes. . . . This is also a special day for the proclamation of the word. Hearing this word proclaimed and explained within the context of the worshiping assembly is decisively different than personal "Bible study" or "knowing what the Bible is about." One would hope that this principle would be self-evident to Christians, especially those from liturgically-oriented traditions. However, sometimes it is not and it needs, therefore, some comment and discussion.

First, in the Roman Catholic Church in the northern hemisphere there is the emerging issue of "priestless Sundays," even in those regions where this was not formerly a problem. The use of this term, however, is problematic because it conceals another deeper problem—"eucharistless Sundays." One hopes that the problem will be alleviated soon. To risk less frequent Sunday eucharists is to risk much of the eucharistic praxis at the heart of the tradition of Catholic worship.

Second, the problem of preparation of and by the various liturgical ministers (for example: the presider, deacon, lectors, cantors, and so forth) arises. These ministers should channel their energies into sound preparation for the Sunday eucharist, especially in comparison with daily eucharist/liturgy. Too often, much time and energy are spent on preparation for celebrations of the eucharist by small groups on days other than Sundays. Where numbers of priests exist the celebration of the eucharist takes place for the slightest of reasons. This might certainly be appropriate on occasion but it should not be the standard liturgical fare. Such daily eucharists should never usurp the centrality of the Sunday eucharist.

Finally, in preparing for weekday celebrations of the eucharist **simplicity** should reign. There should be some discernible difference in solemnity between a weekday and a Sunday celebration of the eucharist. Weekday celebrations of the eucharist often bear great resemblance to Sunday celebrations, give or take a few texts. (Perhaps what is needed is an appropriate weekday eucharistic rite.)

Texts. The liturgical and theological character of any celebration which occurs during Ordinary Time will be colored by its texts and placement within the broader liturgical year. Sunday and weekday celebrations which occur during Ordinary Time are different from those which occur during other liturgical seasons. Seasonal Sunday and weekday celebrations are colored by the season in which they occur. Celebrations during Ordinary Time, however, do not as yet possess such a specifically seasonal overtone. Thus, the liturgical texts of any given celebration during Ordinary Time assume an even greater weight than the liturgical texts of the seasons.

In the United States the character, theme and tone of the Sunday eucharist during Ordinary Time often arise from the three lectionary readings. In a number of other countries the sacramentaries contain special opening prayers composed in light of the gospel readings, a practice that reiterates this emphasis on the readings. The Sunday lectionary is divided into a three-year cycle. The gospel of Matthew dominates in Year A; Mark, in Year B; and Luke, in Year C. For the most part, each cycle is a semi-continuous reading from the gospel. The first reading (from the Hebrew scriptures) has generally been chosen in reference to the gospel reading. Each responsorial psalm has been chosen as an appropriate response to the first reading. There is, therefore, a certain coherence about the gospel reading, the first reading, and the responsorial psalm. The second reading is usually a semi-continuous reading from some New Testament writing. This reading has not been chosen with a specific reference to the gospel passage. Thus, it is difficult (and wrong) to try and force a common theme into all three readings. Sometimes a common theme will be present and sometimes it will not. For example, the lectionary texts for Year A of the Fourteenth Sunday of the Year are:

Reading I:　　Zechariah 9: 9–10. Your king comes to you
　　　　　　　　meek and humbly.
Psalm:　　　Psalm 145. I will praise your name for ever,
　　　　　　　　my king and my God.
Reading II:　Romans 8:9,11–13. You are in the Spirit.
Gospel:　　　Matthew 11:25–30. I am gentle and humble
　　　　　　　　of heart."

One can see here that the first reading and the gospel reading harmonize. Likewise, the responsorial psalm highlights the Zechariah image of "king." The second reading, however, is part of a continuous reading from Romans and does not necessarily lend itself to an immediately harmonized theme.

The weekday lectionary is structured quite differently. The weekday lectionary does not immediately derive from Sunday. A two-year cycle applies to the first reading and responsorial psalm (known as "Year I" and "Year II"). The gospel reading, however, works on a one-year basis. Thus, while we hear the same gospel reading each year, we hear the first reading every other year. Also, the first reading and gospel have not necessarily been chosen with the principle of harmony in mind. For example, examine the following chart illustrating the lectionary readings for both Years I and II for the fifth week of Ordinary Time:

First Reading		Gospel
Year 1	*Year II*	
Genesis 1: 1–19	1 Kings 8: 1–7, 9–13	Mark 6: 53–56
Genesis 1: 20–2, 4	1 Kings 8: 22–23, 27–30	Mark 7: 1–13
Genesis 2: 5–9, 15–17	1 Kings 10: 1–10	Mark 7: 14–23
Genesis 2: 18–25	1 Kings 11: 4–13	Mark 7: 24–30
Genesis 3: 1–8	1 Kings 11:29–32, 12:19	Mark 7: 31–37

The attempt at providing a semi-continuous reading on weekdays can readily be seen when these texts are charted in this fashion. The aim of this revised lectionary is to place before the Christian community a broader portion of the scriptures so that these might be more deeply appreciated and treasured.

Another factor which cannot be overlooked here is the place of non-liturgical annual celebrations vis-à-vis the liturgical year. Great care and discernment must be exercised here. On the one hand an uncritical absorption of non-liturgical celebrations by liturgical planners and assemblies is dangerous. A Christian community must be careful about the possibility of celebrating distorted ideologies. On the other hand, liturgical puritanism can be equally dangerous. For example, to exclude the recognition of the celebration of Mother's Day from a Sunday liturgy is to risk alienating an assembly, not to mention the lost opportunities for the appropriation of valid and traditional sensitivities about motherhood.

PASTORAL ISSUES

Music. In the actual preparation of Sunday eucharistic liturgies for Ordinary Time, music is often a major issue. At times it is unfortunately the only major issue.

The purpose in mentioning music here is to recall some rather important principles in the preparation of liturgical music for use at Sunday eucharist. Here two important documents from the Bishops' Committee on the Liturgy in the United States offer important insights for those who have care for the preparation of Sunday eucharistic liturgy: *Music in Catholic Worship* (revised, 1983) and *Liturgical Music Today* (1982). The principles mentioned here, however, are not simply a reiteration of these documents, but are, rather, general principles which have emerged in the light of some of the practical difficulties associated with the choice of liturgical music in worshiping assemblies.

1. *Avoid songs which more properly belong to the domain of devotion rather than liturgy.* There is a distinction between "liturgy" and "devotion." Liturgy is the church's public (official and communal) prayer. Devotion is by nature a privatized prayer form (though it may certainly take place publicly, communally, and with the approbation of ecclesial authority). For example, in the realm of music the following kinds of songs are inappropriate for liturgy: "God and me" songs, overly sentimental songs, and songs with poetic lyrics which are inaccessible to the community at large.

2. *In general the liturgy should not be "thematized" by the use of song texts.* Remember: the basic themes of the liturgy are praise, thanksgiving and petition/intercession. Where it is decided to employ some sort of secondary theme, care must be taken to insure that the theme emerges from within the liturgical texts and contexts. A theme should not be imposed from outside the liturgy.

The importance of consulting the established liturgical texts must once again be noted here. The various texts of the liturgy often interact dialogically in the process of interpreting one another. It sometimes happens, for example, that the text of a song which has been incorporated into the liturgy without any consultation of the proper liturgical texts actually becomes the textual focus of a given liturgy. This dynamic is somewhat questionable.

General songs of praise and thanksgiving (especially scriptural texts) are appropriate throughout Ordinary Time. Songs which celebrate the place of Sunday and/or various Sunday analogues are obviously appropriate on Sundays. For example, the following text is from the song "On This Day, The First of Days." It is one which (with some alteration) might serve nicely for any given Sunday during Ordinary Time:

On this day, the first of days
God the Father's name we praise;
Who, creation's Lord and spring,
Did the world from darkness bring.

On this day th' eternal Son
Over death his triumph won;
On this day the Spirit came
With the gifts of living flame.

Father, who did fashion me
Image of thyself to be,
Fill me with thy love divine,
Let my ev'ry thought be thine.

Holy Jesus, may I be
Dead and risen here with thee,
And upon love's fire arise
Unto thee a sacrifice.

Spirit, who all gifts impart,
Shine and dwell within my heart;
Best of gifts, thyself bestow;
Make me burn thy love to know.

God, the one God of my Heart,
I am thine, and mine thou art;
Take me, blessed One in Three,
Here I give myself to thee.

Certainly one might criticize both the "God and me" and patriarchal overtones of the language. However, the point here is to note and appreciate the various Sunday analogues which are present: the day of creation, the day of resurrection, the day of the Spirit's coming.

3. *Avoid cluttering the liturgy of Sundays and Ordinary Time*

with music to the detriment of the other liturgical arts. Too much
music may (and often does) become an obstacle to prayer. Liturgy
can become too cerebral and verbose. Remember the other elements of liturgy: gesture, smell, taste, touch, and silence.

4. *The more one can break away from written texts, the better.*
With all due respect, much hymnody which developed from the
Reformation on is actually foreign to Roman eucharistic liturgy. It
tends to tie the community to a book and this changes the experience of liturgy for the community at large. Liturgy becomes something you *read.* Where possible, singing without written texts should
be encouraged. Singing might then be able to move more readily
from prayer of the head to prayer of the heart. Thus, *songs which are
easily remembered and sung are best.* (This, of course, is not a call
for childish songs. Much of the recently published Taize music is
excellent for liturgical participation.) Also, *music which is good
should be repeated . . . and often.* There is a tendency at times to
turn the call for variety into some absolute unharnessed principle.
Variety, however, is not always the spice of liturgical life. Sometimes
it can be a nuisance. Quality songs can and will sustain interest and
enthusiasm even when used often.

5. *The community's taste is important in the choice of songs.*
Because I (or "we"—usually meaning "this particular liturgical
team") like a song is not the best reason for planning its use. Likewise, because I or "we" do not like a song is not the best reason for its
exclusion.

6. *A "Pithy" Guide to Music at Eucharist.*

ENTRANCE SONG/GATHERING SONG:
The purpose of this song is twofold. It accompanies the entrance of the presiding priest and other liturgical ministers. It
also helps to "gather" the community. As such, it is a song
which disposes the community to liturgical prayer.

PENITENTIAL RITE:
Unless the liturgy is a particularly festive one in which there is
much singing, the penitential rite should be musically modest.
It is a simple acknowledgment of our graced but sinful selves

before God and each other, and our need for forgiveness and mercy.

The Kyrie is a litany which acclaims the Lord and asks for healing and mercy. By design it is not the place to list our individual or collective sins.

GLORIA:
The Gloria is a hymn of praise. As a rule it should be sung.

RESPONSORIAL PSALM:
The responsorial psalm is, as its name suggests, a psalm (or scriptural canticle). It is not another reading nor is it a hymn. It should be sung and is best done so in a responsorial fashion.

GOSPEL ACCLAMATION:
This acclamation should always be sung!

CREED:
In a sense the creed is an affirmation of faith which arises from the liturgy of the word. This is a creed, not another song. Generally it should not be sung.

PRESENTATION/PREPARATION OF GIFTS:
This is not an "offertory" time. The offering comes during the eucharistic prayer. If a song is used it should not suggest sacrificial offering. Silence or instrumental music is best at this time.

EUCHARISTIC PRAYER ACCLAMATIONS:
These are: the initial dialogue (The Lord be with you. And also. . .), the *sanctus, "the mystery of faith,"* and the great Amen. As a rule these should always be sung on Sundays and more festive occasions.

OUR FATHER:
Generally this prayer should be sung when prayed in common. Use chant—slow and meditative.

SIGN OF PEACE:
Singing and instrumental music should be avoided. The presumption is that the entire community (including instrumentalists) is offering a sign of peace. We are sharing Christ's peace, not singing about it.

BREAKING OF BREAD:
Breaking bread is one of the major actions of the eucharist. The "breaking of the bread" was one of the names by which many of our earliest ancestors in faith referred to eucharist. The Lamb of God is a litany which accompanies the action of breaking bread and the pouring of the cup. It should last for the duration of that action.

COMMUNION SONG:
This is a processional song sung by an assembly on pilgrimage. It should be easy to remember and simple to sing. IT IS NEVER AN ADORATION SONG!

MUSIC AFTER COMMUNION:
As a rule there should be no singing after the distribution of communion. This is best used as a time of deep communal silence.

RECESSIONAL SONG:
This is an option. The community has already been dismissed.

One might wonder why we should bother worrying about the shape of music here. The pastoral reality, however, suggests that music is a major constitutive element used to celebrate liturgy during Ordinary Time. (Unfortunately it is often the only element attended to, and sometimes rather poorly.)

Focus/"Themes." The danger involved in the importation of foreign themes into the liturgy has been noted elsewhere. This, however, is not to suggest that Sunday and weekday eucharists during Ordinary Time should have no focus. It must always be recalled that the fundamental themes of the eucharistic liturgy are already established: praise, thanksgiving and intercession. The importance of the sacramentary and lectionary texts must be noted. Focus emerges from these essential texts. It is not grafted onto them.

At the same time the community and those who prepare its liturgy must take note of con-texts and extra-liturgical factors which sometimes contribute to the determination of a focus. For example, it is somewhat dangerous to ignore celebrations such as Mother's Day and Father's Day. Where these are incorporated into the eucharist care should be taken to respect the essential texts of the eucharist. Recognition of these celebrations can be drawn responsibly into the homily, the intercessions, and the final blessing. "Theme" Sundays (for example, "Mission Sunday" or "Vocation Sunday") must be carefully scrutinized, but not necessarily ignored. For example, to take up a collection for the missions on Mission Sunday without due liturgical attention to this theme may render the liturgy-mission relationship tenuous. Even strictly secular themes are ignored with great risk. To do so is to run the risk of splitting liturgy from the real-life concerns of the broader community.

In discussing focus it must be remembered that Ordinary Time spans thirty-three or thirty-four weeks throughout the year. Different weeks and/or series of weeks may lend themselves to varying foci. For example, in the northern hemisphere the seasons can greatly influence one's experience of liturgy. Ordinary Time during the winter is experienced differently than during the summer. Weather is a factor which helps determine the way people experience celebrations, and this includes liturgical celebrations. Furthermore, the liturgical texts also offer hints as to variation in focus. For example, the liturgical texts of the last weeks of Ordinary Time lend themselves to an exploration of various eschatological themes.

Color. With regard to color the General Instruction of the Roman Missal (hereafter GIRM) simply notes that "Green is used in the offices and Masses of Ordinary Time" (GIRM #308c). Those feasts of the Lord which are celebrated on Sunday (depending on the region) use their own proper liturgical colors.

This might appear to be a somewhat rigid approach to liturgical colors during Ordinary Time. There are, however, several important points to be made. First, there is something to be said for a consistency of color during Ordinary Time. The use of color is not simply incidental. In most cultures color is a bearer of meaning. Second, the use of green in the Latin church has a long history. Its association with hope (thus, eschatological overtones) is well-known. Third, there are many possibilities in terms of varying shades of green. The shades of green might be coordinated in terms of the actual seasons (Winter, Spring, Summer, Autumn). Fourth, there is more to a vestment than simply color. There is also texture, design, and so forth. These other dimensions should not be over-looked. Finally, while the discussion of liturgical colors takes place within the context of the discussion about vestments in GIRM, other liturgical decorations (for example, colored hangings) should not be overlooked. Together all these can contribute to a total liturgical environment.

Environment. As has been mentioned, the question of liturgical environment should not be simply reduced to the cut and color of vestments. The whole liturgical environment must be attended with great care. On the one hand a certain tasteful simplicity should prevail. On the other hand a boring blandness should be avoided. Any consideration of the liturgical environment should be rooted in an acquaintance with the 1978 document from the Bishops' Committee on the Liturgy, ***Environment and Art in Catholic Worship.***

In considering the type of total liturgical environment which might prevail during the various Sundays and weekdays of Ordinary Time a number of issues should be discussed. Among these are some of the following:

1. What is the rank of the liturgical celebration? Celebrations of simpler rank should be accompanied by simpler liturgical environment.

2. What is the importance and relevance of any given liturgical celebration to a given community? For example, there will be times when a liturgical celebration of optional rank will have greater significance for certain communities. A parish whose patron is St. Bede the Venerable may (and hopefully will) wish to mark the occasion in a more festive manner than one which is not so named. A parish may also wish to mark any given Sunday of Ordinary Time in a

more festive manner as a result of some special parish event which is taking place.

3. What is the natural season of the year? The various seasons of the year lend themselves to differing liturgical environments. A parish, for example, may opt for a relatively simple environment during the summer months. During the autumn months autumn colors might be used. And so forth.

4. What are the central liturgical symbols? The liturgy itself tends to remind the community that the assembly, the altar, and the lectern are crucial focal points. The liturgical environment should be arranged in such a way that these focal points are enhanced. This usually calls for "less rather than more." Liturgical decorations should not become distractive to the assembly's primary purpose for gathering.

5. What are the community's places of devotion? Though devotion is not to be equated with liturgy, nevertheless devotional places are often part of the total liturgical environment. Examples of such devotional places are the place of reservation for the blessed sacrament and shrines in honor of Mary and/or various saints. Care should be taken to insure that these places are both beautiful and tasteful.

One should also remember that in certain communities there are periods which are associated with devotional dynamisms. For example, in many Roman Catholic communities the months of October and May continue to be times during which Mary, the mother of Jesus, figures prominently. It can be dangerous to ignore these dynamisms.

6. What are the civil and secular events which are taking place? For example, in the United States it is common for most people to celebrate Memorial Day. It has become a secular sort of All Souls/All Saints Day. To completely ignore such a celebration within the liturgical arena can be dangerous. The liturgy is certainly an appropriate place to remember those who have suffered and died for legitimate national, international and intra-national values. Again, care must be taken regarding the manner in which such a celebration is liturgically shaped. Cluttering the liturgical environment with

United States flags may bespeak an ideological stance which is actually alien to the liturgy. The Christian community must be conscious of the importation of distorted ideologies to the liturgy.

Saturday Evening Mass. This name itself is problematic and tends to highlight a fundamental pastoral problem with the notion and practice of Sunday eucharist celebrated on Saturday evening.

The problem emerges at that point where the Roman Catholic community understands and designates time itself. The basic problem is that it involves a sudden (and perhaps contrived) shift in telling time. Suddenly the Roman Catholic community is encouraged to think in a Jewish time concept (that is, sunset to sunset), whereas for the remainder of the week it thinks in a traditionally Roman time concept (that is, midnight to midnight).

The practice of celebrating Sunday eucharist on Saturday evening is now prevalent throughout the United States. While Saturday evening eucharists may be imbued with a vigil tone, parish communities must be sure that these eucharists are in fact celebrated as full Sunday eucharists rather than convenient services for those who want "to get mass in" before the weekly Saturday night outing.

Weekday Liturgies. The various liturgical books do not refer to the weekdays by their secular names (Monday, Tuesday, Wednesday, and so forth). It has been suggested that the pagan source of these names is the reason at root here. The GNLYC simply states that the "days following Sunday are called weekdays" (#16). Liturgical books refer to these days as *feria,* meaning "fair day." Certainly this title brings out the special dimension of all time which has been taken up into Christ.

Ferial days during Ordinary Time do not at present possess their own particular prayer texts. There are, however, six prefaces designed especially for use on weekdays. The themes of these prefaces are (taken from their titles in the American sacramentary): all things made one in Christ, salvation through Christ, the praise of God in creation and through the conversion of man and woman, praise of God is God's gift, the mystery of Christ is proclaimed, and salvation through Christ. It is customary in many places to use the prayer texts from the previous Sunday at weekday celebrations of the eucharist. However, there are any number of possible options in this area. GIRM notes that on the weekdays of Ordinary Time the prayers at eucharist may be taken from any of the thirty-four Sunday mass formularies, the mass texts of an optional memorial, the mass texts of a saint listed in the martyrology for that day, a mass for various occasions, or a votive mass (GIRM #316c). It also specifies that when choosing texts "the spiritual good of the faithful" should be considered and that the imposition of the priest's own particular tastes should be avoided (GIRM #316c). This is wise advice, indeed!

There are two important principles to note here. First, weekday eucharistic liturgies should be marked by a certain simplicity. Weekday eucharists are not simply Sunday eucharists scaled down. They do not enjoy the same plethora of theological and liturgical analogues that are intrinsic to Sunday eucharist.

The various options which are possible for weekday eucharists should also be noted. GIRM states that: "On the weekdays in Ordinary Time, the priest may choose the weekday Mass, the Mass of an optional memorial, the Mass of a saint inscribed in the martyrology for that day, a Mass for various needs and occasions, or a votive Mass" (GIRM, 316d). Whatever one may think about the priest as the one who chooses (perhaps he might consult others?), the point here is that there are options which are available and which are often overlooked with regard to liturgical prayer texts.

Lectionary texts, however, are another matter. The weekday lectionary is based on a cycle of continuous readings. The one(s) responsible for the choice of options should be careful about disrupting this cycle. Regarding this matter GIRM notes that "these readings are for the most part to be used on the days to which they are assigned" (GIRM, 319).

It was mentioned earlier that it became customary in many places to dedicate certain days to various persons, truths or devotions. With the exception of Saturday the GNLYC does not mention these. With regard to Saturday it notes that: "On Saturdays in Ordinary Time when there is no obligatory memorial, an optional memorial of the Blessed Virgin Mary is allowed" (#15).

In addition to daily celebrations of the eucharist (where this is possible), a community might entertain the possibility of celebrating the Liturgy of the Hours. "Liturgy," after all, is not simply a synonymn for "eucharist."

SOLEMNITIES AND FEASTS OF THE LORD ON SUNDAY DURING ORDINARY TIME

There are a number of solemnities and "feasts of the Lord" which are celebrated during Ordinary Time. Some of these take place on Sunday. Again, this is not to undermine the importance of Sunday in itself. The GNLYC states that: "Because of its special importance, the Sunday celebration gives way only to solemnities or feasts of the Lord" (#5). Among those which always take place on Sunday are Trinity Sunday (the Sunday after Pentecost Sunday) and the feast of Christ the King (the last Sunday of Ordinary Time). In the United States the feast of the Body and Blood of Christ also takes place on the Sunday after Trinity Sunday.

It is rare that those solemnities and feasts which are immovable fall on Sunday. However, at times this will happen. (For example, during 1990 the solemnity of the Birth of John the Baptist [June 24] fell on a Sunday.)

The Sundays of Advent, Lent and Easter are never to be dislocated by such celebrations (see GNLYC #5). When this happens the celebration of the solemnity or feast is moved to the preceding Saturday. (Again, for example, during 1990 the Annunciation of the Lord [March 25] fell on a Sunday during Lent. It was, however, celebrated on Saturday, March 24.)

The "fixed" solemnities of the liturgical year are:

Solemnity of Mary (Octave Day of Christmas)—January 1
Epiphany—January 6 (or on the Sunday falling between
        January 2 and January 8)
Joseph, Husband of Mary—March 19
Annunciation of the Lord—March 25
Birth of John the Baptist—June 24
Peter and Paul, Apostles—June 29

Assumption—August 15
All Saints—November 1
Immaculate Conception—December 8
Christmas—December 25

The four "movable" solemnities (that is, solemnities that are not tied to a particular calendrical date) are:

Holy Trinity (Sunday after Pentecost Sunday)
Body and Blood of Christ/Corpus Christi (Sunday
    after Trinity Sunday)
Sacred Heart (Friday following the Corpus Christi)
Christ the King (last Sunday of Ordinary Time)

A number of the immovable solemnities will be discussed in subsequent chapters. Here we will deal briefly with those three movable feasts which are celebrated on Sundays in the United States: Holy Trinity, Body and Blood of Christ, and Christ the King.

Holy Trinity. A growing emphasis on a liturgical celebration in honor of the Trinity probably arose as a result of the christological and trinitarian controversies of the fourth and fifth centuries. As a result of these controversies both liturgical and devotional celebrations in honor of the Trinity began to grow in various regions. However, a universal feast in honor of the Holy Trinity was not promulgated until 1334. One of the reasons why such a feast was resisted by Rome entailed the observation that every Sunday (as well as every liturgical day) was at root a celebration of the Trinity.

One of the interesting dimensions of some of the liturgical texts for this feast is their heavy theological quality. For example, in the preface for the feast we pray: "You have revealed your glory . . . three Persons equal in majesty, undivided in splendor, yet one Lord, one God, ever to be adored in your everlasting glory." The texts themselves tend to be rooted in a polemical concern for an orthodox statement regarding the Trinity. In this sense they speak more to the intellect than to the heart.

While such a feast may certainly be criticized (precisely because every Sunday is a celebration of the Trinity), the Christian community does need at times to highlight certain dimensions of belief. This is but one of those instances.

Body and Blood of Christ. The roots of this feast are found in the cult of the blessed sacrament which originated in the twelfth century. It entered the universal calendar in 1264. It is generally held that St. Thomas Aquinas is responsible for the liturgical prayer texts which are used.

There are two caveats which are in order here. First, one must be careful to recognize that this is a feast in honor of the body and blood of Christ. Though the American sacramentary entitles the feast ***Corpus Christi*** ("The Body of Christ"), the Latin ***Missale Romanum*** (Roman Missal) entitles it ***Corporis Et Sanquinis Christi*** ("The Body and Blood of Christ"). The prayer texts are quite clear in this regard. For example, in the opening prayer we pray: "May our worship of this sacrament of your body and blood . . ." In the prayer over the gifts we pray: "Lord, may the bread and cup we offer . . ." In the prayer after communion we pray: "Lord Jesus Christ, you give us your body and blood in the eucharist . . ." Second, one must remember that every celebration of the eucharist is a celebration of the body and blood of Christ.

Another interesting element about the opening prayer and the prayer after communion is that they are addressed directly to Jesus Christ. This is one of the few places where these prayers are directly addressed to Jesus Christ. Within the liturgy we generally pray through Jesus Christ, rather than to Jesus Christ.

In some countries the Solemnity of the Body and Blood of Christ is a holy day of obligation and is celebrated on the Thursday after Trinity Sunday. In the United States it is not a holy day as such, and has been transferred to the following Sunday (see GNLYC #7).

Christ the King. The Solemnity of Christ the King is of recent vintage. The feast was instituted by Pope Pius XI in 1925. Prior to the present reforms it was celebrated on the last Sunday of October. This Sunday was chosen because of its proximity to the feast of All Saints, the kingship of Christ being reflected in the witness of their lives. Similar to Trinity Sunday, the feast of Christ the King has not been without its critics who (correctly) have noted that every liturgical celebration is a celebration of the kingship of Christ. However, it is legitimate to highlight and celebrate certain images of Christ. Furthermore, the feast has been given a different texture in the present calendar.

In the reformed calendar the feast has been moved to the final Sunday of Ordinary Time—this being the Sunday before the Advent-Christmas-Epiphany cycle. While some have suggested that the feast reminds the community that Christ is the goal of each year, it seems that its texts and placement suggest a more forcefully universal eschatological underpinning. The American sacramentary titles the feast "Christ the King." The *Missale Romanum,* however, titles the feast "Domini Nostri Iesu Christi Universorum Regis" ("Our Lord Jesus Christ, King of the Universe"). Christ reigns for all time and over the entire universe! This universality is beautifully expressed in the liturgical prayers. In the opening prayer we pray: "Almighty and merciful God, . . . you make all things new in your Son Jesus Christ, the King of the universe. May all in heaven and earth acclaim your glory and never cease to praise." Again, in the prayer after communion we pray: "Lord, you give us Christ, the King of all creation, as food for everlating life."

The feast is located between the final days of Ordinary Time and the opening days of the Advent-Christmas-Epiphany cycle. These days are imbued with strong eschatological overtones. The Solemnity of Christ the King is not so much the "end" of the liturgical year as it is a transitional point highlighting the eschatological nature of the Christian understanding of time.

A final note—some have suggested that the continued use of "king" as an image for Christ (as well as a metaphor for God) is somewhat problematic. It tends to be overly imperialistic, patriarchal and hierarchical. There is some truth to these observations.

EMBER AND ROGATION DAYS

One rarely hears about "ember" or "rogation" days anymore. In the former calendar the title "ember days" was given to the Wednesday, Friday and Saturday of the four weeks which marked the shift from one season to another. Their origin is most likely related to the agricultural society from which they initially emerged. These were days of prayer, fasting, almsgiving and thanksgiving for the seasonal harvests. The rogation days took place during the Easter season. These days were associated with litanies and prayers of supplication. Their presence in the Easter season was an unfortunate witness to the breakdown, not only of the whole Lent-Easter-Pentecost cycle, but also to a breakdown within the Easter season itself. These litanies and prayers of supplication were usually prayed in processions. One took place on April 25 and a series of others took place on the three days prior to Ascension Thursday.

Though ember and rogation days are no longer designated by those terms, in principle the GNLYC has retained them. It states: "On rogation and ember days the practice of the Church is to offer prayers to the Lord for the needs of all people, especially for the productivity of the earth and for human labor, and to give him public thanks" (GNLYC #45). The conferences of bishops are to arrange for the timing and planning of these celebrations (GNLYC #46).

The "Appendix to the General Instruction for the Dioceses of the United States of America" notes that days should be set aside for prayer for "the fruits of the earth, prayer for human rights and equality, prayer for world justice and peace, and penitential observance outside Lent." It leaves the decision up to the local bishop.

For Personal Reflection and/or Group Discussion

1. Do you think that Ordinary Time is an adequate term by which to understand those Sundays and weekdays which do not possess a seasonal (for example, Advent-Christmas-Epiphany) or festal (for example, feasts of the Lord) character? What alternative terms might be used?

2. A number of the mainline Protestant denominations continue to refer to Sundays in Ordinary Time as Sundays "after Epiphany" and "after Trinity Sunday" (for example, the Lutheran and Epis-

copal Churches). Should the Roman Catholic Church in the United States adopt such designations for ecumenical purposes?

3. Examine the eight prefaces for use on the Sundays of Ordinary Time. In how many of these is the paschal mystery explicitly mentioned? What is the liturgical theology of Sunday which is found in these texts?

4. Do you think that Sunday has lost its uniqueness as a special day and/or as "the Lord's day" among Christians of the West? How might families reappropriate this day?

5. How might the Christian community/parish enhance the celebrations of Sunday liturgically? Do any of the parishes in your area celebrate the evening prayer from the *Liturgy of the Hours?* Do you think it is realistic to hope that Christian communities might reassemble on Sunday evenings for prayer?

6. Do you think that it is appropriate to admit themes into the liturgy which, strictly speaking, are non-liturgical? If so, what might be some examples of non-liturgical themes and/or celebrations which might be recognized and celebrated in the liturgy?

7. Check the sacramentary (or your missal) for a listing of the masses and prayers for various needs and occasions, and votive masses. Page through these and familiarize yourself with the many possibilities which exist. What masses might you add if you had the chance? Why?

4

The Lent-Easter-Pentecost Cycle

An ancient legend recounts how the devil tried to get into heaven by pretending to be the risen Christ. The devil, being a master of disguises, took with him a contingent of demons made up as angels of light and shouted up at the gates of heaven, "Lift up your heads, O ye gates; and be ye lift up, ye everlasting doors; and the king of glory shall come in." The angels looked down on what they thought was their king returning in triumph from the dead. So they shouted back with joy the refrain from the psalm, "Who is the king of glory?" Then the devil made a fatal mistake. In every particular save one he was just like Christ. When the angels in heaven thundered, "Who is the king of glory?" the devil opened his arms and said, "I am!" In that act of arrogance he showed the angels his outstretched palms. There were no wounding marks of the nails. The angels of heaven refused to let the imposter in.

ALAN JONES, *PASSION FOR PILGRIMAGE*

HISTORICAL BACKGROUND

As has been noted elsewhere present research into the development of the liturgical year indicates that the weekly Sunday celebration preceded the annual cycle. By the end of the second century, however, many Christian communities celebrated two annual festivals: the feasts of *Pascha* and *Pentecost.* The mysteries celebrated in the feast of *Pascha* are comparable to those which are today celebrated in the paschal triduum. The festival of *Pentecost* was a fifty-day period of celebration which followed *Pascha.* During this fifty-day period neither fasting nor kneeling was permitted as both were considered to be signs of penitence. Also, during this fifty-day celebration no one particular day (for example, Ascension) was celebrated as such. The entire fifty-day period celebrated the whole mystery of Christ's Pasch and it culminated with the feast of Pentecost on the fiftieth day. The title of this celebration, *Pentecost,* along with some of its themes were probably carried over by the early Jewish Christians from Judaism into Christianity. At the time of the emergence of Jewish Christianity the Jewish feast of Pentecost celebrated (among other things) the giving of the Law. In the early Jewish Christian communities this celebration came to celebrate the outpouring of the Holy Spirit on the church. (It must be remembered that from one theological and liturgical perspective this whole complex could be referred to as simply Pentecost, inclusive of all dimensions. For example, in John 20 the Spirit is given on the day of resurrection, suggesting the unity of these mysteries.)

The celebration of Ascension as a particular day developed in the vicinity of Antioch around 380 C.E. Its initial celebration was probably rooted in the Acts 1 reference which notes that Jesus appeared among his apostles for "forty days" after the resurrection. Acts 1 also provides a description of the "ascension." (See Acts 1:1–11 which is the first lectionary reading for the feast of the Ascension in years A, B, and C. For the gospel references see Mark 16:19 and Luke 24:50–51.) Again, one must not underestimate the symbolic overtones of the number "40." Interestingly enough, the emergence of a separate feast celebrating the ascension of Jesus on the fortieth day after Easter was a catalyst in the eventual fragmentation of this entire period. One of the challenges of the present liturgical-year reforms is to reappropriate the integrity and unity of the entire Lent-Easter-Pentecost cycle, especially the place of Ascension and Pentecost as Easter celebrations.

Lent. The preparatory time which we have come to call Lent was an even later development. Initially the Christian community prepared for the period of the fifty-day festival with fasting and penance. However, this fasting and penance possessed baptismal overtones since this was also a time during which catechumens were prepared for initiation. These two periods—that of fasting/penance and that of the fifty days—were separated by the paschal vigil eucharist. For those Christians already initiated the fasting was anticipatory of the Pasch and lasted for one or two days. With time the period of fasting was extended to one week. This week commenced with a reading of the passion. During the fourth century this period of fasting was further lengthened. At first it became a three-week preparation but it quickly developed into a forty-day period. From the sixth century daily eucharist appears to have been celebrated during Lent on Monday, Tuesday and Saturday. The forty-day sojourn of Jesus in the desert became the prime analogue for understanding entrance into the catechumenate and Lenten period (though certainly others existed such as the forty-year journey of the Israelites in the desert and Moses' forty-day stay on Sinai). With time and the demise of the adult catechumenate, some of the important elements of the Lenten period were lost (for example, many of the baptismal overtones). Among these were its essential alignment with the Easter-Pentecost mysteries, the anticipatory dimension of the triduum fast, and the baptismal roots which were so central to its originating focus.

The actual title by which this time is popularly referred to, "Lent," is actually derived from an Anglo-Saxon word meaning "spring." Lent was associated with the experience of seasonal change from winter to spring, especially the experience of the lengthening of days. It is interesting to note that in the Latin missal (*Missale Romanum*) this period is called **Tempus Quadragesimae,** that is, the "forty-day period of time."

At present the Lent-Easter-Pentecost cycle consists of the forty days of Lent, the paschal triduum, and the fifty days of Easter. Two other periods are also observed during this time: "Holy Week" (which will be discussed briefly in the section on the triduum) and the Easter "octave" (the eight-day period beginning with Easter Sunday). Traditionally this octave period was a time of continued liturgical celebration and catechetical instruction for the newly initiated catechumens. These are no longer emphasized as readily as they once were.

GENERAL PRINCIPLES

Unity. Lent-Easter-Pentecost is best understood as one cycle possessing its own special emphases and dynamisms. The integrity of the Lent-Easter-Pentecost cycle is often obscured in some preaching and popular practice. In many places Lent is celebrated as a forty-day penitential time leading into "Holy Week," the Easter celebration consists of Easter Sunday alone, and the solemnities of the Ascension and Pentecost are grafted on to Easter in a forty-day/fifty-day relationship. Ironically, Lent becomes the lengthiest and most important period in all this. This breakdown in the relationships of the Lent-Easter-Pentecost cycle celebrations has had devastating consequences for a proper understanding of the theology and liturgies of this cycle.

It is important to emphasize the essential integrity of the Lent-Easter-Pentecost cycle. In popular catechesis it might be helpful to move toward speaking about this cycle as one "ninety-day" period. One period ought not to be understood as totally isolated from another. Lent is not simply a negotiable preparatory time. The Easter mysteries consist of more than simply the resurrection of Jesus. Pentecost is more than the descent of the Holy Spirit fifty days after Easter. Lent cannot fully be appreciated and understood apart from Easter-Pentecost, and so forth.

The following chart illustrates the way that communities often *actually understand and experience* this cycle, in contrast to the way in which the liturgical reforms envision understanding and experience of Lent-Easter-Pentecost.

PROBABLE POPULAR EXPERIENCE	HOPED LITURGICAL EXPERIENCE
ASH WEDNESDAY	Ash Wednesday
MEATLESS FRIDAYS	Penance Prayer Almsgiving

Sunday Eucharist	First Sunday of Lent (Election)
	Second Sunday of Lent
	Third Sunday of Lent:
	  First Scrutiny
	Fourth Sunday of Lent:
	  Second Scrutiny

PROBABLE POPULAR EXPERIENCE	HOPED LITURGICAL EXPERIENCE
	Fifth Sunday of Lent: Third/Final Scrutiny
PALM SUNDAY	Passion Sunday
[Holy Thursday]	PASCHAL TRIDUUM Mass of Lord's Supper
GOOD FRIDAY	Good Friday
Holy Saturday Vigil	Holy Saturday Vigil
EASTER SUNDAY	Easter Sunday Evening Prayer
	Easter Octave—"Feasts"
	(Period of Mystagogy) Easter Sunday Second Sunday of Easter Third Sunday of Easter Fourth Sunday of Easter Fifth Sunday of Easter Sixth Sunday of Easter
Ascension Thursday	Ascension Thursday Seventh Sunday of Easter
Pentecost	Pentecost

Note the differences. People often experience the cycle as a series of isolated celebrations while the reforms envision a certain unity. The one season which often is experienced as a unity, Lent, is experienced as such more because of practices such as meatless Fridays, "sacrifices" ("giving up" things), and Stations of the Cross, than because of its liturgical celebrations. The reform, however, suggests that there is a coherence and unity during these ninety days. Furthermore, the reforms understand baptism/initiation as a common thread weaving these days together. The First Sunday of Lent is a time for "election" of those adults to be initiated at the vigil. The

Third, Fourth, and Fifth Sundays of Lent are days of "scrutiny" for the elect/catechumens. The Holy Saturday vigil is a time for the initiation sacraments for the elect/catechumens. The Easter season is a time for mystagogical catechesis for the newly initiated. The local community journeys with the elect/catechumens and newly initiated through all this. Thus, the Lent-Easter-Pentecost cycle is a communal journey rather than a journey of private asceticism.

This, of course, is not to suggest that the different times and celebrations of the Lent-Easter-Pentecost cycle are simply interchangeable and similar to one another. Nor is it to suggest that there is a certain predetermined individual faith response which is called forth by the cycle. Lent has its own emphases (for example, fasting-abstinence and penance), as do Easter and Pentecost. Rather, the different emphases must be understood and appreciated in the light of one another. The GNLYC notes some of the following:

Lent. Lent is a preparatory time (#27). This does not mean that it is secondary in some negotiable way. Rather, Lent moves the community toward Easter-Pentecost. It is both a baptismal and penitential time (#27). In the parish context this is readily seen in terms of the preparation of catechumens for initiation (as well as the reconciliation of those who have been alienated from the ecclesial community).

Lent lasts from Ash Wednesday to the "mass of the Lord's Supper" on Holy Thursday (#28). The mass of the Lord's Supper is part of the paschal triduum and not part of Lent strictly speaking (#18). It should also be noted that Sundays are considered part of Lent. The GNLYC refers to these Sundays as the Sundays *of Lent* (#30). There is a certain sobriety and somberness about these Sundays. This is suggested by the silencing of the gospel "alleluia" (#28) as well as the absence of the Gloria (GIRM #31). Simultaneously, however, one must keep in mind that these (like all Sundays) are also celebrations of the resurrection. While one may speak about the sobriety of these Sundays, "penance" ought not be allowed to be the prism through which these days are understood and celebrated.

Easter-Pentecost. Easter-Pentecost (the "Easter Season") consists of the fifty days from Easter Sunday to Pentecost Sunday. This fifty-day period is meant to be celebrated as one great feast. The GNLYC refers to this fifty-day period as the "great Sunday" (#22).

The first eight days after Easter form an "octave" of Easter and these days are celebrated as solemnities (#24). Furthermore, the solemnity of the Ascension of the Lord Jesus is celebrated (in the United States and certain other countries) forty days after Easter (#25). In some countries the celebration of the Ascension has been moved to Sunday. The celebration of Ascension and Pentecost within the context of Easter is a liturgical and theological statement which should not be overlooked. Ascension and Pentecost are part of the Easter mysteries. For example, in the "Ascension I" preface we pray: "The joy of the resurrection and ascension renews the whole world. . . ." In the opening prayer for vigil mass of Pentecost we pray: "Almighty and ever-living God, you fulfilled the Easter promise by sending us your Holy Spirit."

Baptism. Baptism is at the heart of the Lent-Easter-Pentecost cycle. Lent initially developed as a period during which two primary movements took place: the movement of the catechumens toward the waters of baptism, and the movement of penitents toward reconciliation with the church. The first of these to develop was the catechumenate, the second was the order of penitents. These two movements were related in that reconciliation was understood to be a kind of second baptism. The whole church made this journey with the catechumens and the penitents. The eclipse of an adult catechumenate and the emergence of private confession served to focus this period primarily on those already initiated or reconciled.

For the newly initiated, however, the process did not stop with the celebration of initiation at the paschal vigil. The journey toward initiation issued into the Easter-Pentecost celebrations. There was a certain unity not only about the sacraments of initiation (baptism, confirmation, eucharist) but about this period as a whole. One has only to examine the liturgical texts of the Lent-Easter-Pentecost period (especially those of the Easter octave) to discover the many baptismal themes and references. For example, in the opening prayer for Saturday of the fifth week of Lent we pray: "Protect all who are about to become your children, and continue to bless those who are already baptized." In the opening prayer on the Easter octave Monday we pray: "Help us put into action in our lives the baptism we have received with faith." On Saturday of the third week of Easter we pray: "God our Father, by the waters of baptism you give new life to the faithful." This journey of the catechumens/penitents was not and is not meant to be undertaken independent of the remainder of the community. Historically both the initiation of the catechumens and the reconciliation of penitents were *public* and *communal.* The ecclesial community moved with them, not separated from them.

This common journey is envisioned in the present reforms. The ecclesial community makes the journey with the catechumens remembering the grace of conversion and baptism. (This, of course, presumes that there are catechumens to be initiated and possibly penitents to be reconciled.) One cannot fully appreciate the theology of this cycle without some familiarity with and appreciation for the *Rite of Christian Initiation of Adults* (RCIA). We all approach the waters of baptism during the Lent-Easter-Pentecost cycle either for the first time as a catechumen or in memory of our own initiation.

The relationship between the RCIA and the Lent-Easter-Pentecost cycle is highlighted in the following diagram:

LENT-EASTER-PENTECOST CYCLE	RITE OF CHRISTIAN INITIATION OF ADULTS
Ash Wednesday	
First Sunday of Lent	Rite of Election
Second Sunday of Lent	
Third Sunday of Lent	First Scrutiny
Fourth Sunday of Lent	Second Scrutiny
Fifth Sunday of Lent	Third Scrutiny
Passion Sunday	
Holy Thursday	
Good Friday	
Holy Saturday/Paschal Vigil	Sacraments of Initiation
Easter Sunday	
Second Sunday of Easter	

LENT-EASTER-PENTECOST CYCLE	RITE OF CHRISTIAN INITIATION OF ADULTS

Third Sunday of Easter
Fourth Sunday of Easter
Fifth Sunday of Easter
Sixth Sunday of Easter
Seventh Sunday of Easter
 	
Pentecost Sunday
	Masses for Neophytes
	  throughout Sundays of Easter
	  with mystagogical catechesis

The Cycle C gospels in the lectionary also bring out the penitential and reconciliation nature of this time (and thus, our journey with penitents). The gospel for the Third Sunday of Lent is Luke 13—the fig tree episode; the gospel for the Fourth Sunday of Lent is Luke 15—the prodigal son story; the gospel for the Fifth Sunday of Lent is John 8—the woman accused of adultery.

Paschal. The whole Lent-Easter-Pentecost cycle is a celebration of the paschal mystery. There is a tendency to isolate the different dimensions of the paschal mystery and to assign each dimension to a different time of the Lent-Easter-Pentecost cycle. Lent becomes a time to concentrate on the suffering and death of Christ, Easter becomes a time to celebrate the resurrection of Jesus, and so forth. This becomes problematic when the various dimensions of the paschal mystery are torn asunder and when the essential unity of the cycle is lost. It further causes the meaning of the various times and celebrations of the cycle to become too securely anchored. The texts of the Lent-Easter-Pentecost cycle are imbued with a sense of the whole paschal mystery. In the prayer over the gifts for Ash Wednesday (the first day of the Lent-Easter-Pentecost cycle) we pray: "By this sacrifice may we be prepared to celebrate the death and resurrection of Christ our Savior. . . ." Also, in the Lent I preface we pray: "Each year you give us this joyful season when we prepare to celebrate the paschal mystery with mind and heart renewed." The liturgical year is not some sort of family album which the Christian community takes out each year to admire old photographs. We do not celebrate Lent in the pretense that the resurrection has not yet happened. Likewise we do not celebrate the resurrection forgetful of the suffering and death of Christ in the past and in the present. The suffering, death and resurrection of Christ is an ever-present reality, especially in the lives of the suffering, poor, oppressed and marginalized. The cross is neither a fashion accent which one wears around a neck or on a lapel, nor is it a product that the ecclesial community is trying to sell with all the aggressive gimmickry of Madison Avenue.

Bishop Henri Jenny in *The Paschal Mystery in the Christian Year* defined Lent as "the annual renewal of the whole Church in the Paschal Mystery by means of the sacraments." As definitions go this is a good one. Bishop Jenny's specification of sacraments is certainly helpful. The definition, however, sins by its confinement. What Jenny says here about Lent should in actuality be said about the whole Lent-Easter-Pentecost cycle.

Prominence. Within the Christian cycle of seasons and feasts the Lent-Easter-Pentecost cycle possesses a certain prominence. In its section on the yearly cycle the GNLYC first considers the importance of the triduum (#18–21). It speaks about the triduum as the culmination of the entire liturgical year (#18). The ramifications of this statement will be discussed at a later point. What is of interest here is the fact that after considering the triduum the GNLYC goes on to discuss the Easter season and Lent (#22–31). Subsequently it discusses the Christmas season, Advent, Ordinary Time, and rogation and ember days (#32–47). This arrangement suggests two things. First, the Lent-Easter-Pentecost cycle is theologically and liturgically central in the liturgical year. Second, Lent must be understood within the context of Easter-Pentecost.

Central Symbols. The theology of the Lent-Easter-Pentecost cycle is expressed in the central symbols of this cycle. These should not be overlooked. There are a number of symbols and symbolic actions which emerge as expressive of the theology of this cycle. These should be employed as fully as possible. Among the symbols are: ashes, palms, cross, water, light and paschal candle. Among the symbolic actions are: foot washing, cross kissing, candle lighting, water bathing and palm carrying. There is also the significant image of desert journeying which underpins Lenten time. All these present themselves as central symbols, actions, and images of the cycle and should be treated as such. Attention should be paid to the ways in which these symbols, actions, and images function to empower the community. One suspects that if attention were given to these central symbols, actions, and images the community would not have to search out and focus attention on secondary and additional (not to mention sometimes alien) programs and services. Only after these central dynamics have been given a prominent place and fullest possible expression should the community look for other ways to celebrate this cycle.

Texts. Attend to the liturgical texts of the cycle. Once again this principle must be emphasized. While the central symbols, actions and images must be allowed to emerge, it would be dangerous to do so oblivious of the liturgical texts which accompany this cycle. This is true for both the particular celebrations within the cycle as well as for the texts of the cycle taken as a whole.

In reflection on and preparation for Lent-Easter-Pentecost look at phrases and texts which are found throughout the cycle, especially those having to do with *baptism, paschal mystery,* and *penance.* These offer hints about the liturgical theology which underpins the cycle. It must also once again be emphasized that *all the texts* should be allowed to speak. One should not simply look to the lectionary texts. It is especially during this cycle that the other prayer texts (presidential prayers, entrance and communion antiphons, and so forth) act as a prism through which the paschal mystery is proclaimed and celebrated.

PASTORAL ISSUES

Ash Wednesday. Ash Wednesday remains an immensely popular day for Catholic Christians. This is the first day of the Lent-Easter-Pentecost cycle, one on which Catholics enter into the cycle by being marked with ashes. This custom, which is rooted in the ancient Hebrew penitential practices of wearing sackcloth and ashes, was first adopted by the church as part of a ceremony of expulsion of public and notorious sinners. At the beginning of Lent public sinners were expelled from the church using the text of Genesis 3:19—"Remember, you are dust and unto dust you shall return." This expulsion from the church was associated with the expulsion of Adam and Eve from paradise. The text highlighted the association between the expulsion, sin and death. Eventually it came to be practiced by the entire Christian community on Ash Wednesday.

The present sacramentary notes that the ashes used should "come from the branches blessed the preceding year for Passion Sunday." The liturgical prayer texts for Ash Wednesday suggest some of the following notions: struggle against evil, self-denial, repentance, and works of charity. There are two possible formulae for use during the marking with the ashes. The first is a new, more positive and gospel-oriented one: "Turn away from sin and be faithful to the gospel" (Mk 1:15). The second is the former one: "Remember, you are dust, and unto dust you shall return" (Gen 3:19). In many places the traditional formula is no longer used because of negative overtones. This may represent a real loss considering the original context from which it emerged. Its images are powerful.

Many liturgical ministers bemoan the large crowds which appear for ashes, but perhaps the popular persistence of Ash Wednesday practices presents liturgical ministers with tremendous possibilities for catechesis.

Penitential Acts. The practice of engaging in certain penitential acts during Lenten time has been customary for many Catholics. The liturgical prayer texts for Lent are filled with references to penance and discipline. For example, in the prayer after communion on Ash Wednesday we pray that "through this communion may our Lenten penance give you glory. . . ." As a matter of record the practice of receiving ashes on Ash Wednesday along with the practice of "giving up" some thing or some act have often been the main constituents of Lenten understanding and undertaking for many Catholics. This probably continues to be the case for many people. These practices, however, ought to be contextualized so that they might be better understood.

Generally speaking, it is within an understanding of Lent as a time of movement toward deeper conversion and the waters of baptism (as well as a time for the reconciliation of public—or not so public—sinners) that one might come to a better understanding of the penitential acts that are performed. These acts are not performed simply to gain the favors of an arbitrary God nor the forgiveness of a wrathful God. (Please note that no judgment is being made here regarding favor or forgiveness as motivation for certain penitential practices.) Rather, penitential acts might be better contextualized within the dynamisms of conversion and confrontation with the power of evil. Lent is a time when those professing the Christian faith through the initiation process, those who had been lost to the ecclesial community of faith and now seek reconciliation, and finally, those who have learned in faith that both initiation and reconciliation are signs that move us *all* toward the future, seek conversion. Those to be initiated or reconciled are not divorced from the rest of the community.

The Second Vatican Council called for a type of penance that is not only "internal and individual but also external and social" (CSL #110). This call is certainly not a denial of individual and personal forms of penance. These are quite appropriate. Salvation, though communal, is always personal.

By the same token, however, salvation, though personal, is also communal. The church is the body of Christ. We are saved as a people. Jesus is never my personal savior in isolation from the community at large. Both the personal and communal dimensions of this salvation in Christ ought to be expressed by appropriate penances which are signs of authentic conversion. Furthermore, as communal, such penitential practices ought also have a broader social implication. We are not saved as isolated communities either. Communal penances with broader social implications can be works on behalf of both mercy and justice.

Where common penances with social implications are undertaken it might be good if the whole group (or some representative portion of a community) joins in the decision-making process regarding the concrete form of the penance. This allows a community to "own" the penitential practice. Common penances sometimes fail because the community at large has had little to say in the matter. They are sometimes imposed by an individual or some tiny segment of the community. Ideally a common penitential practice should neither be handed down from on high nor contrived by a minority group which might be unrealistically overdosing on one ideology or another.

One caveat is in order here. The acts of penance undertaken by the individual and the community ought also possess a "mystical" character; that is, such acts ought to be signs of surrender to God and be directed primarily toward a relationship with the mystery of God as that mystery calls us to conversion. Penitential acts are not necessarily subtle social programs. The Second Vatican Council noted that "the real essence of the virtue of penance is hatred for sin as an offence against God" (CSL #109). Sin is not simply to be understood in terms of its social consequences alone. For example, penitential practices ought not simply be fashionable means by which money is raised for the poor (though such a project might certainly involve deprivation of one sort or another). The raising of money for the poor belongs more properly to the Lenten practice of almsgiving. If all this sounds complex, it is. Penitential practices involve the mystical, personal, communal, internal, external and social.

One must also remember that "penance" is but one dimension of the traditional Lenten triad—prayer, fasting and almsgiving. In the prayer over the gifts on Ash Wednesday we pray: "Lord, help us to resist temptation by our Lenten works of charity and penance." Also, in the opening prayer for the Third Sunday of Lent we pray: "Father, you have taught us to overcome our sins by prayer, fasting and works of mercy." Penance must also be combined with prayer and almsgiving.

Music. Those who plan the music for this cycle should strive for hymns and songs which are theologically sound and liturgically appropriate. For example, during Lenten time songs with a negative anthropology should be avoided. "O God, I'm scum. Let me slither in your presence" lyrics have no place in Christian liturgy. We are not scum and God made snakes to slither. The issue here is not the presence of penitential themes and practices. The GNLYC (#27) notes that penitential practices which are baptismally oriented are quite appropriate. Rather, the issue here is a negative anthropology. Some Lenten "penitential" songs and practices can border on this type of anthropology and these songs are best left forgotten.

With regard to song texts it is best to explore those which carry forth the baptismal, reconciliation, and conversion themes. This raises a caveat: Avoid selecting songs simply because they happen to appear in the Lent, Easter, or Pentecost section of the hymnal. Check other sections of the hymnal for songs which are appropriate to the Lent-Easter-Pentecost cycle.

Below are a few points which might be helpful in planning music for this cycle.

1. Strive for simplicity, especially during Lenten time. The ***Ceremonial of Bishops*** notes that during Lent "the use of musical instruments is allowed only to support the singing" (#252). However, this first involves the simplification of normal singing patterns. Every liturgical gathering during Lent does not require the use of another song about prayer, fasting, almsgiving, and so forth.

Learn a select number of quality songs with good theological bases and sound liturgical underpinnings and use these with some regularity. A few well-chosen songs, hymns, and antiphons should be able to carry a community through Lent as well as Easter-Pentecost.

After singing patterns have been simplified then move toward simplifying the musical accompaniment during Lent. Where possible explore singing without accompaniment, taking into account the size and talent of a community. At a minimum avoid (or curtail) the use of instrumental music during Lent. This is a good way to differentiate Lenten time from Easter-Pentecost. A few well-chosen songs and more and deeper silence can help move individuals and communities toward deeper conversion.

Music should not be made to bear the whole burden for conveying the meaning and significance of this cycle. There are many other ways to convey its meaning and significance.

2. Avoid excessive "thematizing" of the liturgies of the Lent-Easter-Pentecost cycle. As has already been noted the basic themes of the cycle are already set down in the liturgy. If one wants to seek the themes of the cycle consult the sacramentary and lectionary before consulting the parish hymnal. One should especially consult the opening and communion antiphons when choosing entrance and communion songs. This again brings into focus the caveat regarding the imposition of secondary and/or alien themes and ideologies which the cycle may or may not sustain. Such themes should emerge from, not be imposed on, the liturgy.

3. When planning the repertoire for the Lent-Easter-Pentecost cycle, keep the essential unity of the cycle in mind. This is not to suggest that there is not a difference in Lent, Easter, and Pentecost songs, nor is it to suggest that any and every song contained in the

Lent, Easter, Pentecost section of the hymnal can be used at any given time during the Cycle. Some songs are clearly Lenten in themeology while others are more Easter-Pentecost; however, the unity should not be eclipsed. As a rule the liturgical music of this cycle *should be planned as a whole.*

Passion (Palm) Sunday. Passion (Palm) Sunday remains an immensely significant day in the lives of many Catholics. As the official title contained in the sacramentary ("Passion [Palm] Sunday") indicates, there are two emphases in the celebration. On the one hand we celebrate Christ's triumphant entry into Jerusalem. On the other hand we celebrate the passion of Christ. The model greeting for the presider contained in the sacramentary brings together these two emphases: "Christ entered in triumph into his own city, to complete his work as our Messiah: to suffer, to die, and to rise again." The relationship between the palms and the passion ought not be eclipsed. As the *Circular Letter Concerning the Preparation and Celebration of the Easter Feasts* (hereafter CLEF) indicates: "The connection between both aspects of the paschal mystery should be shown and explained in the celebration and catechesis of this day" (#28). The mass texts of the day, however, give clear emphasis to the passion. As a matter of fact the presidential prayer texts mention neither the palms nor the triumphal entry of Christ into Jerusalem. They focus clearly on the suffering and death of Christ.

Easter's Fifty Days. The GNLYC notes that "the fifty days from Easter Sunday to Pentecost are celebrated in joyful exaltation as one feast day, or better as one 'great Sunday'" (#22). From a pastoral perspective the celebration of Easter's fifty days is somewhat problematic. It is difficult in today's world to sustain a celebration over such a long period of time. This period is a **festival time** for the Christian community, yet we generally do not celebrate fifty-day festivals in modern western society. Furthermore, this festival period is often interrupted by other celebrations (first communions, confirmations, marian celebrations during May, graduations, and so forth) which tend to collapse its integrity and meaning. When one adds the actual lapse of time the celebrations of Easter Sunday, Ascension, and Pentecost Sunday one begins to see the possibilities for tearing asunder the theological and liturgical unity of the fifty-day Easter festival.

There are a number of pastoral questions which must be addressed by the whole community (and not simply those who plan the liturgical celebrations). How can the liturgical and theological integrity of the whole Lent-Easter-Pentecost cycle be appropriated and sustained? More particularly, how can the liturgical and theological unity of the fifty-day Easter festival be supported and maintained? How might a community incorporate other celebrations (if possible) into the celebration of the fifty days of Easter in such a way that they help sustain it?

This last question is a crucial one. It is unlikely that other celebrations (first communions, confirmations, marian May celebrations, graduations) are going to be eliminated. Furthermore, it is not the contention here that they need to be eliminated. The concern here is that they be celebrated in such a way that they are understood through the prism of the Easter festival and not in isolation from it.

Extra-liturgical Celebrations. Extra-liturgical celebrations have long been a dimension of the Lent-Easter-Pentecost cycle. One need only look at the past popularity of the "Stations of the Cross" to realize this. There is no need to eliminate such extra-liturgical celebrations, but they should be planned and celebrated in the spirit of the Lent-Easter-Pentecost cycle. They are not meant to replace or counteract the liturgy. The CLEF notes: "Devotional exercises that harmonize with the lenten season are to be encouraged, for example, 'The Stations of the Cross'. They should help foster the liturgical spirit with which the faithful can prepare themselves for the celebration of Christ's paschal mystery" (#20). In preparing such devotional celebrations one must always keep their secondary nature in view.

In this process the sacramentary and lectionary might help as springboards for ideas regarding the shape and content of extra-liturgical services. For example, one rich resource which is often overlooked is the "Office of Readings" for the Liturgy of the Hours.

In the process of preparing such celebrations the creative appropriation of past traditions and practices ought not be overlooked. There are quite a number of fine versions of the "Stations of the Cross" which have been written and published in recent years. Furthermore, with some creative redesigning certain elements of the old ***Tenebrae*** service might be reappropriated for use during Holy

Week. The traditional eucharistic devotion known as "benediction" might also contain possibilities. The idea espoused here is to creatively envision new forms of eucharistic reverence which might be appropriate within the context of the Lent-Easter-Pentecost cycle.

Liturgy of the Hours. It might be helpful to briefly recall some of the points which ought to be operative here:

1. The hymn texts for celebrations of the Liturgy of the Hours need not be specifically "Lenten" or "Easter." The readings and other proper texts can bear this burden.

2. Entertain the possibility of incorporating appropriate non-scriptural and non-liturgical readings and texts. (However, the scriptural and liturgical texts should be neither eclipsed nor replaced.)

3. Choose one or two particular books of the scriptures to be read continuously.

4. In parishes and communities where the Liturgy of the Hours is prayed regularly this might be a good time to move away as much as possible from reliance on books. Use books only when and as *needed.* The liturgy should be neither exclusively cerebral nor wedded to books in such a way that one can be frustrated when attempting prayerful engagement.

For Personal Reflection and/or Group Discussion

1. Examine the various prefaces used during Lent. There are actually twelve in all (4 general prefaces, 5 prefaces for the Sundays of Lent, 2 prefaces for the "Passion of the Lord," and 1 for Passion [Palm] Sunday). What do these prefaces express concerning the meaning and celebration of Lent?

2. Do you think that people continue to experience the marking with ashes on Ash Wednesday as a significant part of their liturgical and spiritual life? Do you think that Christians experience this as a real call to conversion or simply as a cultural ritual in which they engage because "that's what we've always done on Ash Wednesday"?

3. Examine the two ascension prefaces contained in the sacramentary. What is the theological understanding of the ascension con-

tained in them? How do these texts connect the mysteries of the resurrection and the ascension?

4. Do you think that people actually perceive the mysteries of the ascension and Pentecost as Easter mysteries? Why or why not?

5. Examine the lectionary and sacramentary texts for Passion (Palm) Sunday. What is the theological and liturgical meaning of the day which the texts yield? Do you sense that there is a dichotomy between the emphasis of the texts for the "Commemoration of the Lord's Entrance into Jerusalem" and the mass texts? Which emphasis (palm or passion) seems to be more significant in your own experience? In the experience of other people?

6. Should penitential acts always have a social implication (for example, "giving up" some item so the money saved can be used for the poor)?

7. Is there any attempt in your parish/community to convey the unity of the Lent-Easter-Pentecost cycle?

8. The devotion known as "Stations of the Cross" has traditionally consisted of fourteen stations. The fourteenth station was "Jesus is placed in the Sepulcher." More recent versions have added a fifteenth station, "The Resurrection." What are the theological implications of this addition? Do you think it is appropriate?

5

The Paschal Triduum

Come to the feast, ye heaven of heavens, which as the Spirit
exclaims proclaim the glory of God! (Psalm 19:1);
in that they are first to receive the paternal light of the Divine
*   Spirit.*
Come to the feast, angels and archangels of the heavens,
and all you heavenly host,
As you look upon your heavenly king
come down in bodily form to earth.

Come to the feast, you choirs of stars
pointing out him who rises before the morning star.
Come to the feast, air which extends over the abysses. . . .

Come to the feast, briny water of the sea,
honored by the sacred traces of the footsteps.
Come to the feast, earth, washed by the divine blood,
Come to the feast, soul of humanity,
aroused by the resurrection of a new birth.
SOURCES CHRÉTIENNES 27.121–123, ED. P. NAUTIN

HISTORICAL BACKGROUND

The earliest Christian communities did not celebrate a specifically Christian feast of Easter. It was probably not until the early years of the second century that some Christian communities began to do so and even then the church at Rome did not accept the practice until the second half of the second century. The initial annual celebration of *Pascha* appears to have been a unitive celebration. It was one proclamation of the passion, death and resurrection of Christ and the Christian's participation in that mystery through the waters of baptism. The vigil celebration was preceded by a fast on the Friday and Saturday before it but there was no division and historicization of the paschal mystery. Thus, there was no "Holy Thursday" celebration on which the institution of the eucharist and priesthood was celebrated as there was no "Good Friday" celebration focusing exclusively on the passion, crucifixion and death of Jesus.

The original triduum consisted of (Good) Friday, (Holy) Saturday and (Easter) Sunday. It was a unitive celebration in which Christians gathered on Friday to begin a paschal fast of anticipation. This fast was broken by a joyful Easter eucharist at the Great Vigil of Easter. We see, therefore, that many of the elements of our present Easter vigil were there: fasting, assembling of the community, readings from the scriptures, and the celebration of the eucharist. Interestingly enough, what appears to be absent are elaborate baptismal and light ceremonies.

With time the Easter vigil came to be understood as *the* time for the celebration of initiation. The development of the catechumenate was certainly a catalyst here. Ironically, the eclipse of the adult catechumenate also served to signal the decline of the Easter vigil. After the seventh century, when there were no longer many (or any) adult catechumens to be baptized, the "vigil" came to be celebrated during the earlier hours of Holy Saturday. Eventually it was celebrated as early as two o'clock in the afternoon. With this shift much of the meaning of the vigil was eclipsed.

Another dynamic, however, was also at work in reshaping the paschal celebration. Some time during the fourth century the liturgical situation changed. The celebration of the **Pascha** experienced a certain division and somewhat dramatic historicization. Good Friday came to be celebrated as the day of the passion, crucifixion and death of Jesus. It was a day marked by mourning and sorrow. Easter Day came to be the celebration of the resurrection in a way which ignored the death of Jesus. Thus, liturgically (and theologically) the passion and death of Jesus were disconnected from the resurrection. Eventually the notion of Christ's Pasch was reduced to the celebration of the resurrection at the Easter vigil and/or at the Easter Sunday liturgy. This separation had other ramifications as well. For example, the idea and practice of the paschal fast of Friday and Saturday were eclipsed and came to be absorbed by the Lenten penitential fast.

By the time of Amalarius of Metz (775–852) the triduum days were Holy Thursday, Good Friday and Holy Saturday. This was an interesting development because Easter Sunday itself came to stand outside the triduum. The Pasch itself (now understood as celebrated on Easter Sunday) ironically came to be located outside the paschal triduum. Furthermore, after the ninth century there was the emergence of a second "triduum"—Easter Sunday, Easter Monday and Easter Tuesday.

The present rebirth of the celebration of the paschal vigil actually preceded the reforms of the Second Vatican Council by two decades. The revision began as an experiment in 1951 and was given final approbation in 1955/56. After centuries of celebrating the "vigil" on Holy Saturday morning, the Ordo of 1951 made it clear that the ideal time for its celebration was in the middle of the night. The celebration of the Easter vigil mass should not begin before midnight (though the Ordo did allow the ceremonies to be moved back to earlier evening hours). Among other reforms were the simplification of the rites to allow for popular participation, the blessing of the fire outside the church and in the midst of the faithful, the reduction of the readings from twelve to four (of course, whether this reduction was a positive step forward might be debated), and the celebration of baptisms and/or renewal of baptismal promises.

The most recent reforms of the vigil contained in the Missal of 1970 reflect a further revision of the 1951 Ordo. Perhaps the greatest revision is an attempt to once again appreciate the fundamental liturgical and theological unity of the whole paschal triduum. Among the reforms which touch upon the vigil are: a flexible approach to the time of the vigil, the relocation of the baptismal liturgy after the homily, and a flexibility with regard to the number of scripture readings. Below is a comparative chart illustrating the structure of both the 1951 and 1970 vigils.

1951 Ordo	*1970 Ordo*
The Rite of Fire	The Service of the Light
Blessing of paschal candle	Blessing of fire
(Procession)	Preparation/lighting of candle

1951 Ordo	1970 Ordo
Exsultet	Procession Exsultet
The revival of baptism The lessons Genesis 1 and 2	The Liturgy of the word Invitation to listen to the word Seven Old Testament readings —at least 3 should be used
Exodus 14:24–15:1	—Exodus 14:15–15:1 must be used
Isaiah 4:2–6	—prayers after each reading
Deuteronomy 31:22–30 —each followed by prayer —last three readings followed by scriptural song	
The Litany of Saints (Part I) Blessing of water Baptism	Gloria Collect Epistle reading (Romans 6:3–11)
Procession to font with water	Solemn Easter Alleluia Gospel
Renewal of baptismal vows The Litany (Part II— Be merciful, spare us. . . .)	Homily
The eucharistic celebration Begins With Kyrie Collect First lesson—Col 3:1–4 Meditation song—Psalm 117 Second lesson—Matt 28:1–7 Prayer over gifts Eucharistic prayer Communion song—Ps 22:1–6	The liturgy of baptism Prayer for those to be baptized (Blessing of font) Litany of saints Blessing of baptismal water Renunciation of sin/profession of faith Baptism-Confirmation Renewal of baptismal promises

1951 Ordo	1970 Ordo
Lauds—Ps 150 & Lk 1:68–79	Sprinkling of assembly
Concluding prayer	General intercession
	Liturgy of Eucharist

In the present liturgy the paschal triduum consists of the period of time from the celebration of the evening mass of the Lord's supper through evening prayer on Easter Sunday. Thus, the triduum actually consists of the evening of Holy Thursday, Good Friday, Holy Saturday, and Easter Sunday up to evening prayer.

GENERAL PRINCIPLES

Paschal Mystery. The paschal triduum celebrates the life, passion, death, and resurrection of Jesus Christ, and our incorporation into that mystery. The paschal triduum is not simply the celebration of the "Easter" mystery of resurrection. It looks to the whole of Christ's life, passion, death, and resurrection. To reduce the triduum (or any one of its celebrations) to simply one dimension of this whole mystery is to impoverish it beyond proper theological and liturgical recognition. The liturgical prayer texts reveal this richness. For example, the entrance antiphon for Holy Thursday is Galatians 6:14: "We should glory in the cross of our Lord Jesus Christ, for he is our salvation, our life and resurrection; through him we are saved and made free." In the opening prayer of Holy Thursday we pray: "He (Christ) gave it (the supper/eucharist) when he was about to die. . . ." In the first prayer during the "Celebration of the Lord's Passion" on Good Friday we pray: "Lord, by shedding his blood for us, your Son, Jesus Christ, established the paschal mystery."

Furthermore, the paschal triduum (like all liturgy) is neither a matter of recalling nor repeating the past. The liturgy does not simply mimic. We ourselves are drawn into the reality of the mystery being celebrated. For example, in the prayer following the reception of communion at the Good Friday celebration of the Lord's passion we pray: "May we who participate in this mystery (the triumphant death and resurrection of Christ) never cease to serve you (Almighty and eternal God)." During the paschal triduum it is most necessary to be aware of this as these are often celebrations which yield a strong temptation toward historicization.

Eschatological. The paschal triduum is an eschatological celebration. The triduum looks toward the Second Coming of Christ. This eschatological dimension is particularly proper to the vigil celebration. The CLEF states that "the full meaning of vigil is a waiting for the coming of the Lord" (#80). This eschatological dimension, therefore, is not rooted so much in the texts of the vigil as in the context—that is, the very dynamic of keeping vigil, not only for the resurrection but for the Second Coming of Christ.

Though in a veiled fashion, some of the liturgical prayer texts of the triduum do bring out this eschatological dimension. For example, in the preparation of the candle during the vigil Christ is spoken about as the "beginning and the end, Alpha and Omega." During the Exsultet we pray: "May the Morning Star which never sets find this flame still burning."

Interestingly enough, the early Christian communities believed that the Lord Jesus would return during the celebration of the paschal vigil. This was one important reason why they actually kept vigil.

Culmination. The paschal triduum is the culmination of the *entire* liturgical year. It is sometimes said and thought that the paschal triduum is the heart of the Lent-Easter-Pentecost cycle. This, however, is a partial truth. The GNLYC states clearly that the "triduum of the passion and resurrection of Christ is the culmination of the entire liturgical year" (#18). The CLEF reiterates this: "the summit of the whole liturgical year is in the sacred Easter triduum of the passion and resurrection of the Lord" (#2). The celebration of the triduum is to the liturgical year what the Sunday celebration is to the liturgical week.

Again, at the heart of the celebration of this paschal triduum is the notion of *anamnesis* by which we keep the memory of Christ's Pasch in such a way that we are drawn into the mystery here and now. With regard to this keeping of memory two important points must be kept in mind. First, this *anamnesis* is an act of the whole assembly. Second, this *anamnesis* is a dynamic that is operative throughout the whole of the liturgical year as well as during the paschal triduum. We are not attempting to mimic the actions of Jesus as if we were merely recalling past historical facts. For example, the "washing of feet" on Holy Thursday is a ritual action which functions as a kind of "sacrament" rather than simply a reenactment of Jesus' washing of his disciples' feet. What we celebrate in the paschal triduum is neither simply a set of historical facts nor simply a set of dogmatic statements. Rather, we make memory of and celebrate the central mysteries of our Christian faith as expressed in its central stories, symbols and rituals. We are drawn into the paschal mystery by way of the various narratives, ritual gestures (for example, the washing of feet), and the symbols of water, oil, bread and wine.

Integrity. The life, passion, death and resurrection of Jesus Christ is celebrated throughout the entire paschal triduum, which should not be approached as a set of isolated and separate liturgical celebrations. It should be approached as essentially one liturgy with various moments—some of them quite public and communal, others quite personal and individual. When we allow the paschal triduum to collapse into separate and isolated liturgies a certain liturgical dysfunction sets in, the essential unity of the triduum is eclipsed, and its liturgical celebrations become divorced from one another. As a result the liturgical celebrations of the triduum can (and have) become overly historicized. Holy Thursday becomes the day dedicated to celebrating the "institution" of holy orders and the eucharist. Good Friday—and Holy Saturday—become days of mourning on which we recall the passion and death of Jesus. The vigil and Easter Sunday become the time we celebrate the resurrection. Such isolation is theologically dangerous. Furthermore, this kind of overhistoricization allows a questionable hierarchy of importance to slip in (for example, the Saturday vigil is "more important" than Good Friday which is "more important" than Holy Thursday, and so forth).

This is not to suggest that everything is of equal weight and importance. The paschal vigil is the *high point* of the liturgical celebration of the paschal triduum, but not in a way which isolates it from the celebrations of Holy Thursday and Good Friday. Furthermore, one must remember that the Liturgy of the Hours is another dimension of the paschal triduum which is often overlooked in both religious and parish communities.

The following chart indicates the basic liturgical structure of the paschal triduum as envisioned by both the most recent hours and missal reforms:

THE PASCHAL TRIDUUM:

EVENING Mass of the Lord's Supper	GATHERING OF ASSEMBLY 　Gloria WORD WASHING OF FEET CELEBRATION OF LORD'S 　SUPPER transfer of blessed sacrament (quiet stripping of altar) + adoration until midnight +
Good Friday	Morning Prayer Midday Prayer (reassembling in quiet) WORD GENERAL INTERCESSIONS VENERATION OF THE CROSS procession reproaches public veneration COMMUNION (quiet departure)
Holy Saturday	MORNING PRAYER MIDDAY PRAYER (gathering of elect)

EVENING PRAYER

(reassembling in quiet)
SERVICE OF LIGHT
blessing of fire
preparation of candle
procession
easter proclamation
WORD
LITURGY OF BAPTISM
blessing of font
litany of saints
baptism
renewal of promises
confirmation
EUCHARIST

Easter Sunday

MORNING PRAYER
MIDDAY PRAYER
EVENING PRAYER

The structure and dynamisms of the paschal triduum become fairly evident when viewed from such an integrated perspective. The triduum clearly begins with the evening mass of the Lord's supper and continues through evening prayer on Easter Sunday. In its entirety it consists of approximately seventy hours filled with liturgy, private prayer, fasting, reading, resting, vigiling, and so forth. The triduum takes place in private and familial settings as well as within the liturgical context.

PASTORAL ISSUES

Preparation. All major preparations for the paschal triduum should be completed prior to beginning of the evening mass of the Lord's supper on Holy Thursday. The time of the triduum is one of communal and private engagement in the celebration of the paschal mystery. While "on the spot" problems may present themselves and need to be solved, the time of the triduum itself should not generally be cluttered with last-minute changes, music and ritual practices, ritual decisions, and so forth. When all these preparations and practices have been completed beforehand people are freed to enter into the spirit of the triduum (its silence, liturgy, fasting, spiritual reading, and so forth).

Fasting. The fast which is observed during the triduum is referred to as the "Easter fast" (GNLYC #20). It is also known as the "paschal fast." This specification highlights the difference between the fasting during Lent and the triduum fast. The fasting of the triduum is not considered to be an essentially penitential fast. It is, rather, a fasting of "anticipation." It has as its goal not penance, but the preparation of the community to celebrate ever more joyfully the vigil and subsequent Easter-Pentecost time.

Environment. The essential theological and liturgical integrity of the triduum has been emphasized. This integrity should be expressed in the liturgical environment, particularly in terms of the liturgical decorations which are used. If the worship space looks radically different for the various celebrations of the triduum the idea may be communicated that the celebrations have no intrinsic connection with one another. This is not to suggest that the worship space look exactly the same for all the triduum celebrations. Rather, it is to suggest that certain themes should be carried through by the use of some symbols and decorations as common denominators. For example, the use of a special cross (rather than a crucifix) in a place of prominence throughout the whole triduum might be one way to convey this. All indications of the passion and death of Christ should not suddenly disappear at the paschal vigil and/or on Easter morning (when the sanctuary often becomes cluttered with lilies). Christ has moved through death and born his wounds into eternity. Another possible way to convey this is to drape the Easter white (or red on Palm Sunday, Good Friday, and Pentecost Sunday) over the Lenten purple.

Music. There are a number of ways to use music as a catalyst in emphasizing the unity of the triduum celebrations. The first way is by paying some attention to the texts which are found in the sacramentary. Special attention should be given to the entrance and communion antiphons. For example, the entrance antiphon for the evening mass of the Lord's supper on Holy Thursday clearly sets the theme for the whole triduum. This antiphon is an adaptation of the well-known Galatians 6:14 text: "We should glory in the cross of our Lord Jesus Christ, for he is our salvation, our life and our resurrection; through him we are saved and made free." This first liturgical text of the triduum celebration should not be overlooked. It is the door through which the community enters the triduum. The theme of any gathering and an opening song used on Holy Thursday should align itself as closely as possible to this text. One possibility, for example, is the well-known hymn, "Lift High the Cross."

A second way to emphasize the unity of the triduum is by using the same basic acclamations and chants throughout. For example, entertain the use of the same *Sanctus,* eucharistic acclamations, and *Agnus Dei* on Holy Thursday and at the paschal vigil. It might also be possible to use the same chant during the reception of communion on Holy Thursday, Good Friday and the vigil. This text could be one that relates the paschal mystery to the eucharist. (See the communion antiphons for Holy Thursday and the vigil.)

Liturgy of the Hours. As has already been noted, the celebration of the Liturgy of the Hours is part of the celebration of the triduum. From a liturgical perspective the Hours are not something "extra" which are added on or sandwiched in-between the various other liturgical celebrations of the triduum. The Liturgy of the Hours is intrinsic to the paschal triduum. Its texts help further unpack and celebrate the meaning of the paschal triduum.

In light of this parishes and religious communities might give some consideration to the possibility of celebrating some of the Hours in common. At a minimum serious consideration should be given to celebrating evening prayer on Easter Sunday. Remember that the GNLYC notes that it is Easter Sunday evening prayer (not the vigil) that brings the triduum itself to its conclusion.

The Seder Meal. It has become the practice in a number of parishes and religious communities to celebrate the Jewish seder meal. This usually takes place toward the end of Lent, often during Holy Week, and especially on Holy Thursday. While this practice to appreciate our Jewish roots may be useful, it is not without its problems. First, there is the possibility that the Jewish community might not understand what it is that Christians are attempting to do. The seder is a meal which is deeply sacred to and reverenced by Jews. Christians should hesitate to enter into its celebration too lightly. Second, its celebration has built-in theological and liturgical problems. The seder celebrates the Jewish Passover. Christians, however, celebrate their Passover within the context of the paschal triduum, especially the vigil. The passover of the angel of death as well as the exodus is but one dimension of this for Christians, a dimension which has been incorporated into the triduum celebration. One need only refer to the Exsultet to see how some of the Jewish Passover themes have been absorbed and transformed. There is a sense in which celebrating the seder is somewhat redundant for Christians. Finally (especially if the seder is celebrated on Holy Thursday), it would seem appropriate that the community continue efforts to celebrate as best as possible the present triduum celebrations rather than add further celebrations.

If Christians want to celebrate the Jewish seder meal perhaps this would be best accomplished by joining with a Jewish family, Jewish friends, or the local synagogue.

Holy Week. In the reformed liturgy "Holy Week" is itself a strange notion. The GNLYC notes that "Holy Week has as its purpose the remembrance of Christ's passion, beginning with his Messianic entrance into Jerusalem" (#31). Paragraph 31 continues by speaking about the chrism mass. The ***Commentary on the GNLYC*** notes that "Holy week includes the last days of Lent and the first *days* (italics mine) of the Easter Triduum." Yet the Commentary speaks only about Holy Thursday in the context of the blessing of the oils and chrism. The question here is: what are the "first days of the triduum" to which the Commentary refers? The CLEF speaks about "the days of Holy Week, from Monday to Thursday inclusive" (#27). The days appointed here are based on GNLYC #16. The point is that there is some confusion here. At best, what days actually constitute "Holy Week" remain unclear. Furthermore, it is really not a "week" in terms of a seven-day period.

The Sunday prior to the triduum, "Passion Sunday" (more commonly referred to as "Palm Sunday"), as well as Monday, Tuesday, and Wednesday of "Holy Week" are actually days of Lent. Thus, "Holy Week" is not some special unified liturgical and theological celebration. Rather, it is a time consisting of the final days of Lent which act as a transition point into the paschal triduum.

From a pastoral perspective, however, it should be recognized that many (if not most) people tend to think in terms of a "week" rather than a "triduum." The notion of "Holy Week" is still alive and well among many people. In point of fact, the real "triduum" which is often celebrated by Christians during this week is Passion (Palm) Sunday, Good Friday, and Easter Sunday. Though this situation might be lamented it does at least present those who have care of liturgical preparations with an opening. The emphasis on Holy Week might be a door through which people can be encouraged to enter into the celebration of the paschal triduum.

The Chrism Mass. The chrism mass is generally associated with Holy Thursday. There is only one chrism mass and it is often celebrated in the cathedral, though another place which has special significance may be chosen. It is not part of the paschal triduum, strictly speaking, and can be transferred to another day though the day of celebration should remain close to Easter. The chrism and oil of catechumens blessed at this liturgy are used in the initiation sacraments celebrated during the paschal vigil.

The reformed chrism mass involves two rather different celebrations. It is a liturgy which celebrates the blessing of the oils and the consecrating of chrism, and during which priests renew their commitment to priestly service.

The renewal of commitment to priestly service is a rather recent development and has been much criticized as an attempt to change the nature of the celebration into one focused primarily on the ordained. However, the CLEF notes that "the faithful are also encouraged to participate in this Mass and to receive the sacrament of the Eucharist" (#35). There is certainly some validity to criticisms leveled against the reformed chrism mass. However, when and where the faithful do attend, and when and where the faithful do experience their presbyterate to be one of servant-leadership, this celebration can become a deeply moving one. It stands as a challenge to presbyters to move beyond narrow clericalism and to remember who and what is at the heart of priestly ministry.

Passion Readings. It has become both customary and popular in many parishes to read the passion accounts on Passion (Palm) Sunday (Year A–Matthew, Year B–Mark, Year C–Luke) and Good Friday (John) in a drama-like fashion. The gospel is distributed among liturgical ministers, usually with the remainder of the assembly taking the "crowd/people" part. The length of the passion accounts, the limited dramatic abilities of the presider/deacon, and the attention span of the assembly are listed as some of the motivating factors here. This practice, however, is not without its problems and some critical perspectives ought to be raised.

First, there is the temptation to understand the proclamation of the gospel as a kind of dramatic reenactment, a "you were there" episode. We are not there; rather, Christ is here. The gospel proclamation is a reactualization of the passion events within the context of the liturgical assembly. Care must be taken to make sure that the assembly does not understand itself as simply playacting or pretending.

Another problem has to do with the assignment of "parts." The presiding priest usually takes the "Jesus lines," other liturgical ministers (including the deacon) take the commentator and individual lines, and the assembly usually takes the role of the "crowd/people." However, the subtle messages being sent here are in need of rethinking. For example, the assembly becomes the crowd which demands the crucifixion of Christ. Is this association proper? Furthermore, considering the deacon's usual liturgical role in the proclamation of the gospel, it would be rather appropriate for the deacon to take the lines of Christ.

Finally, when lines are assigned to many liturgical ministers and the whole assembly, the entire assembly becomes glued to the reading of a text. Proclamation then runs the risk of becoming an exercise in reading a script. Ironically the assembly is often invited to sit during the gospel (because of its length) thus sending a contradictory message that they are actually an "audience" even though they have a "part."

The issue is not that such practices should be completely abandoned nor that the elderly and sick should be made to stand throughout a lengthy reading. Rather, we need to be alert to critical questions regarding some popular and customary practices and to search out the best possible means for understanding and appreciating liturgical worship.

For Personal Reflection and/or Group Discussion

1. Have you been aware of the eschatological overtones of paschal vigiling? Do you think that the Christian community in general is aware that the vigil is not simply a celebration of the death and resurrection, but also a waiting for Christ's Second Coming?

2. Do you sense that people are aware of the basic unity and integrity of the paschal triduum?

6

The Advent-Christmas-Epiphany Cycle

It is madness to wear ladies' straw hats and velvet hats to church; we should all be wearing crash helmets. Ushers should issue life preservers and signal flares; they should lash us to our pews. For the sleeping god may wake someday and take offense, or the waking god may draw us out to where we can never return.

ANNIE DILLARD, *TEACHING A STONE TO TALK*

There is a birth from God before the ages, and a birth from a virgin at the fullness of time. There is a hidden coming, like that of rain on fleece, and a coming before all eyes, still in the future.

CYRIL OF JERUSALEM, *CATECHETICAL INSTRUCTION 15*

HISTORICAL BACKGROUND

The celebration of a feast in honor of the birth of Jesus did not emerge in the west until the fourth century. Scholars generally note that by 336 C.E. such a feast was in place and celebrated in Rome on December 25. It is difficult to pinpoint with any certainty the exact year that the feast of the nativity was first celebrated in Rome, but the available evidence suggests that it was celebrated for at least a decade prior to 336 C.E.

This comparatively late development of a feast in honor of Jesus' birth, especially because Christmas is so central in the lives of many contemporary Christians, may seem surprising to us today when compared with the Easter triduum. However, this late development is probably indicative of the general eschatological outlook of most primitive Christian communities. These communities awaited an imminent Second Coming. Celebrations such as Christmas would have made little sense to communities that awaited the Lord's return in their own lifetimes. It was only with time and an obviously delayed Second Coming that a celebration such as Christmas could emerge. Furthermore, time provided the opportunity for a greater and more mature theological reflection on the mysteries of the incarnation and the Second Coming.

The reasons for the choice of December 25 (in Rome and its environs) as the date for commemorating the birth of Jesus continue to be discussed and debated. The commonly held theory (sometimes referred to as the "history of religions" theory) is that the date was chosen in reaction to the celebration of the pagan feast of the "unconquered sun-god." Some recent scholarship, however, has contested this hypothesis. The relatively late establishment of the pagan feast (probably around 274 C.E.), as well as other factors suggest that it posed no real threat to the Roman Christian community which would be worthy of a liturgically-based reaction.

A second possible explanation for the choice of December 25 as the feast of the nativity of Jesus (sometimes referred to as the "computation hypothesis") explores the relationship of the nativity feast to that of the annunciation/passion of Christ which was celebrated on March 25. It has generally been thought that the December 25 celebration actually determined the choice of March 25 as the feast of the annunciation. However, the process may actually have worked in reverse. According to a rather ancient tradition Christ was supposed to have died on March 25. While the actual reasons for dating the death of Christ on this day are somewhat difficult to ascertain (it was probably related to the spring equinox), the nativity, annunciation and passion celebrations seem to be related in terms of the computation of their respective liturgical dates. The logic of the early church fathers involved a *symbolic* computation of time. For symbolic reasons it would be unseemly that Christ should not begin and end his life in *whole time periods.* Thus, if Christ died on March 25, then surely the Word was enfleshed in Mary's womb on March 25. From March 25 one calculates forward by nine months to arrive at December 25 as the date of Jesus' birth.

Thus the primitive celebration of the annunciation/passion on March 25 might actually have predated and influenced the choice of December 25 as the celebration of Jesus' birth. Furthermore, there is a certain theological and liturgical propriety in associating the birth of Jesus with his Pasch.

Several significant points should be noted here. First, it is unlikely that December 25 is the actual date of Jesus' birth. This should not stop us from celebrating December 25 as Christmas, nor should it send us into a frenzied search for the actual day of Jesus' birth. The historicity of Jesus' birth is hardly dependent on knowing the actual date and day on which he was born. Second, the process of choosing a date for Christmas was probably more complex than simply a reaction to a particular pagan feast. The process involved in this computation remains somewhat speculative even today. Finally, the issue remains relevant for us today precisely because it reminds us that while we do celebrate a particular historical event, the birth of Jesus of Nazareth, there remains so much more to the Christmas celebration. There is lodged herein a sweep of theological truths which underpin the liturgical commemoration of Jesus' birth on December 25. Grace, sin, redemption, and the destiny of humankind are but some of these truths.

Epiphany and Baptism of the Lord. The feasts of Epiphany and the Baptism of the Lord also factor into this cycle.

The feast of Epiphany most likely developed in the church at Rome after the establishment of the December 25 nativity celebration. However, it was already being celebrated in the churches of Gaul and Spain. This is quite understandable as Epiphany is an eastern feast in origin and both Gaul and Spain evidence early eastern liturgical influences. It was sometime during the fourth century that the feast of Epiphany was adopted in Rome. This adoption involved an adaptation in terms of its focus. Whereas in the east the feast of Epiphany celebrated many of the same themes as Christmas, in its Roman adaptation its focus became the visit of the astrologers (the "magi") from the east and the manifestation of the Christ to them. In the west Epiphany became generalized as a feast which celebrated the manifestation of Christ to the Gentiles.

Originally the baptism of Jesus and the first miracle at Cana were also celebrated on the feast of Epiphany, especially as these events were also considered to be manifestations of the Christ. In the present Roman liturgy the feast of the Baptism of the Lord is celebrated on the Sunday after Epiphany. Its foci are: the manifestation in the Jordan of Jesus as God's beloved Son, the inauguration of Jesus' public ministry, the performance of Jesus' first miracle ("sign") at the wedding feast of Cana, and the call of the Christian community to be faithful to their baptismal commitment.

Advent. In the west a time of preparation also developed in relation to these feasts. We have come to call this preparatory time **Advent.** Its development, too, is complex. It has varied in length as well as meaning from one place to another.

In Gaul and Spain, its focus tended to be the feast of the Epiphany. In these regions baptisms were celebrated on the feast of the Epiphany and this preparatory time was overladen with baptismal and penitential concerns. This preparatory time generally lasted forty days. It was a time of fasting and penance. It came to be known as "St. Martin's Lent" because it began on November 11, the feast of St. Martin. Saturdays and Sundays were not calculated, since these were not considered appropriate days to fast.

There is no evidence of such a preparatory time in Rome until well into the sixth century and its concerns were not baptismal. In Rome it most likely grew out of the practice of observing certain "ember" days (Monday, Wednesday and Saturday) as a preparation for the celebration of the feast of Christmas. It was Pope Gregory the Great (590–604) who established a four-week liturgical preparation for Christmas. Interestingly enough, the Roman liturgical texts of the sixth and seventh centuries suggest that the "coming" of the Lord which the community was preparing to celebrate was that of the birth of Jesus. It was not until the Middle Ages that this preparatory time came to be more forcefully imbued with eschatological themes. This was probably due to the liturgical exchange which took place between Rome and other geographical regions.

THE ADVENT-CHRISTMAS-EPIPHANY CYCLE IN THE LITURGICAL YEAR

On the one hand there exists an essential unity among the various feasts and times of the Advent-Christmas-Epiphany cycle.

On the other hand, these various feasts and times express different foci and are bound by the overall strictures of the liturgical year. This cycle can be outlined as follows:

FIRST SUNDAY OF ADVENT
   (Immaculate Conception—solemnity)
SECOND SUNDAY OF ADVENT
THIRD SUNDAY OF ADVENT
FOURTH SUNDAY OF ADVENT

   (VIGIL OF CHRISTMAS)
CHRISTMAS DAY
   (Stephen, first martyr—feast)
   (John, apostle and evangelist—feast)
   (Holy Innocents, martyrs—feast)
HOLY FAMILY (Sunday within Christmas Octave)
MARY, MOTHER OF GOD, Octave Day—solemnity

EPIPHANY (January 6 or Second Sunday after Christmas)
BAPTISM OF THE LORD (Sunday after Epiphany)

The GNLYC first mentions the "Christmas season" after which it mentions "Advent" (#32–42). The feasts which celebrate the "early manifestations" of Jesus (such as the Epiphany and the Baptism of the Lord) are considered as part of the Christmas season (#37, 38).

The parameters of the Advent-Christmas-Epiphany cycle are set forth clearly. Advent begins with first vespers of the Sunday falling closest to (or on) November 30. The first weeks of Advent give themselves over to a consideration of the Second Coming of Christ (#39). The days from December 17 to December 24 serve as a more direct preparation for the celebration of the commemoration of the birth of Jesus (#42). The Christmas season begins with first vespers on Christmas Eve (#40) and extends until the Sunday after the feast of Epiphany, the "Baptism of the Lord" (#33). This Sunday, like Epiphany, is a *manifestation* feast. Ordinary Time follows on the Monday after the celebration of the "Baptism of the Lord."

An examination of the structure of the Advent-Christmas-

Epiphany cycle suggests three distinct yet related "times." The first of these is Advent with its two varying foci. The second is the Christmas festival which is composed of Christmas and its octave celebrations. These include the feasts of St. Stephen, St. John the Evangelist, the Holy Innocents, the Holy Family, the Solemnity of Mary, Mother of God, and any other remaining octave days (#35). The final period consists of the other manifestation feasts which occur within this cycle: the Epiphany and the Baptism of the Lord.

From this examination there also arise a number of theological, liturgical and pastoral concerns. Several of these concerns have to do with the various marian celebrations which occur during the cycle. How any given community deals with these in the concrete might, and will, vary from one situation to another. They are simply noted here.

Immaculate Conception. From a theological and liturgical perspective the Solemnity of the Immaculate Conception (December 8) is not, strictly speaking, part of this cycle. The date of this solemnity has been determined in relationship to the celebration of the feast of the Birth of Mary on September 8 rather than as a direct theological and liturgical adjunct to this cycle. Its presence within the cycle is more accidental than deliberate. (The GNLYC does not mention this solemnity at all when discussing Advent. Its proper is placed within the sanctoral cycle of the sacramentary. Furthermore, an examination of its prayer texts reveals that no mention is made of Advent, Christmas or their theological themes.)

In light of some contemporary themes in the theology of Mary (especially as contained in some of the liturgical texts for this celebration), the thrust of this feast tends to be ecclesiological. This has prompted some writers to suggest that the celebration of this feast be moved to another date outside the Advent-Christmas-Epiphany cycle. It appears, however, that this will not happen in the immediate future. One author has suggested that the Immaculate Conception, being "the inauguration of the incarnational reality" be celebrated on the Fourth Sunday of Advent.

How a community celebrates this solemnity with its own theology within the Advent season becomes a question. Perhaps some form of accommodation between the theological and liturgical thrust of the feast in itself, and the broader liturgical cycle during which it is celebrated, might seem advisable. The Solemnity of the Immaculate Conception, however, should not simply be transmuted into another Advent celebration because its themes are broader than those of Advent.

Our Lady of Guadalupe. In 1988 the liturgical celebration of Our Lady of Guadalupe was elevated to the rank of "feast" in the United States. This rank is especially important considering how significant this feast is among Latinos in America as the commemoration of Mary's single appearance in North America. It received its own set of particular liturgical texts which must be used. Again, the issue revolves around the way in which the feast can be incorporated into the Advent-Christmas-Epiphany cycle. The person and image of Mary already factor greatly into Advent time. Thus, there exists the risk of allowing Advent to become dominated by the person and image of Mary.

By happy coincidence this feast is celebrated during the opening weeks of Advent. In liturgy and personal reflection it might be helpful to capitalize on some of the eschatological overtones of the liturgical texts for the feast. For example, the entrance antiphon, Revelation 12:1, speaks about "a great sign (which) appeared in the sky, a woman clothed with the sun, with the moon under her feet, and on her head a crown of twelve stars." The prayer after communion exhorts the community to "live united and at peace in this world until the day of the Lord dawns in glory." These blend in quite well with the eschatological thrust of the cycle, especially that of the first two weeks. In addition, the reality of Mary's role in the life of the pilgrim church manifested at Guadalupe could also be a way of focusing this celebration.

Mary, Mother of God. This octave day of Christmas is related to the Christmas festival and is the most ancient marian feast native to Rome. However, in addition to being the feast of the Mother of God, January 1 is also designated as a world day of prayer for peace, and in the civil calendar it is New Year's Day. The celebration of these very different themes on one feast, however, can become an onerous burden. Without falling into the trap of "thematizing" the celebration it seems pastorally advisable to focus the celebration on commemorating Mary, mother of God, while finding creative ways to weave the peace and New Year's overtones into the celebration. Creative persons (especially presiders and planners) might be encouraged to find ways to allow the solemnity to act as a prism through which the gift and burden of a peace-filled New Year can be celebrated.

Holy Family. In most countries today the feast of the Holy Family occurs on the Sunday within the octave of Christmas. While devotion to the Holy Family has been popular in certain countries and regions since the sixteenth century, the feast of the Holy Family has been universally binding only since 1920. There is a sense in which the feast is somewhat grafted onto the cycle. The focus of the texts for this feast tends to be the Holy Family as a model for all other families. The preface for the feast is chosen from among the Christmas prefaces, indicating its Christmas connection. Considering that Christmas-time is a family bonding time for many, its inclusion within this cycle can be mined for its positive dimensions.

Celebrations Outside the Cycle. From a theological and liturgical perspective the celebrations of the Presentation of the Lord on February 2 and the Annunciation of the Lord on March 25 also belong to the Advent-Christmas-Epiphany cycle. The feast of the Presentation belongs to that genre of celebrations referred to as "manifestation" feasts. The feast celebrates the presentation of Jesus in the temple forty days after his birth. The suggested introduction to the feast found in the sacramentary begins by reminding the assembly that "forty days ago we celebrated the joyful feast of the birth of our Lord Jesus Christ." The Christmas connection is immediately made explicit. This feast is also referred to at times as "Candlemas" (coming from "Candle Mass") because candles are blessed before the mass and used as part of the entrance procession. Hence, the Advent-Christmas-Epiphany image of "light" looms large.

The Solemnity of the Annunciation is a feast which celebrates the enfleshment of the Word in the womb of Mary as well as the angel Gabriel's announcement and Mary's *fiat.* There continues to be some question about the theological nature of the liturgical solemnity of the annunciation. In the church's present classification of feasts it is designated as a "feast of the Lord." However, in many places it continues to be celebrated as a feast in honor of Mary. In *Marialis Cultus* Pope Paul VI referred to this feast as a joint celebration in honor of Christ and Mary. Perhaps this ambiguity is good in that it is a reminder that the meaning of any given feast is not necessarily carved in stone.

GENERAL PRINCIPLES

Paschal. The Advent-Christmas-Epiphany cycle is essentially a celebration of the paschal mystery. This principle has already been noted and deserves to be reiterated here. The history of the liturgical year has demonstrated that the Advent-Christmas-Epiphany cycle can readily lend itself to eclipsing its essential paschal relationship. The cycle is too often collapsed into the celebration of the birth of the baby Jesus in Bethlehem two thousand years ago. The paschal mystery, however, reminds the Christian community that it is an adult Christ in his life, death and resurrection who is celebrated even during the Advent-Christmas-Epiphany cycle. This is not to deny that in a particular time and place the Word did, indeed, become flesh. The enfleshment of the Word, however, is more than simply Jesus' birth. The incarnation of the Word is the beginning of the event of our redemption and our divinization which comes to us through Jesus Christ.

A number of the liturgical prayers express this paschal relationship. For example, in the opening prayer of the Fourth Sunday of Advent we pray that God might "lead us through his (Jesus') suffering and death to the glory of the resurrection."

The liturgical prayers of this cycle are rather sparing in their references to a "birth." It is often the "Word" or an adult Christ about whom these prayers speak. When the birth is spoken about it is often in reference to humankind's salvation. Interestingly enough, a number of traditional hymns and carols also point out the connections. See, for example, the second verse of the popular song, "What Child Is This?," or the text of the hymn, "Of the Father's Love Begotten."

The prominence of John the Baptizer during Advent time is a further reminder of this paschal connection. Scripturally, John the

Baptizer is a noted figure in the emergence of the adult Jesus in the public arena. John is associated with the beginnings of Jesus' public ministry. It is not the prenatal John leaping in Elizabeth's womb who is emphasized. It is the prophetic and challenging adult John. It is also important to recall that the figure of the Baptizer participates in bringing the Advent-Christmas-Epiphany cycle to closure on the feast of the Baptism of the Lord.

Also noteworthy from a paschal perspective are the liturgical celebrations on the days immediately following Christmas. These are celebrations of persons who have traditionally been associated with martyrdom: Stephen, John the Evangelist, and the "Holy Innocents." Stephen is known as the first voluntary martyr. John, though not martyred, was ready to give his life. The "Holy Innocents" are also considered to have been martyred for the sake of Christ. (Red is the liturgical color of this day.) These celebraons are ranked as "feasts." Mention should also be made of the optional memorial in honor of Thomas Becket, bishop and martyr, celebrated on December 29. Thus, the martyrial celebrations during the octave of the Christmas festival serve to remind the community of the paschal content of the Advent-Christmas-Epiphany cycle.

The point here is not to try and pin down one or two exact ways in which the Advent-Christmas-Epiphany cycle is essentially paschal in nature, but rather to recognize that there are many ways in which this relationship is expressed and to explore them.

Eschatological. The whole Advent-Christmas-Epiphany cycle is eschatological in its thrust. It is commonplace to note that Advent time (particularly in its first two weeks) is eschatological. This focus, however, while dominant during these two weeks, is not exclusively confined to them. It is present during the whole of Advent time as well as during the whole of the cycle.

This assertion that the Advent-Christmas cycle is eschatological is related to the more fundamental assertion that the whole liturgical year is essentially eschatological in its thrust. During the Advent-Christmas-Epiphany cycle, however, this general eschatological concept is heightened. Many of the texts of this cycle focus on the end times and the Second Coming. For example, in the opening prayer of the Second Sunday of Advent we pray that we might become one with Christ "when he comes in glory." In the opening prayer for December 21 we pray that we might "rejoice in the gift of eternal life when he comes in glory." The liturgical texts from Christmas onward are also imbued with more subtle eschatological overtones. For example, in the opening prayer of the Monday after the Epiphany we pray that we might be led "to the radiant joy of our eternal home." The eschatological overtones of the various Christmas-Epiphany liturgies tend to be more personal. There is a sense that we have not completely arrived. (Perhaps it would be more accurate to suggest that God in Christ has not yet completely arrived.) The Christian community is reminded that it is ever awaiting the coming of God whether in existential grace, in death, or in the consummation of history at the Second Coming.

There is both paradox and tension in this. On the one hand God's coming in the birth of Jesus at Bethlehem is affirmed; on the other hand we yet await the coming of God in Christ at the end of time. An unresolved and paradoxical tension revolves around the simultaneous presence and absence of God. While the mystery of the incarnation reminds of the presence of God, the mystery of the Second Coming reminds us of God's absence. We yet await the future of God in Christ, as well as our future in God.

Incarnational. The whole Advent-Christmas-Epiphany cycle celebrates the mystery of the incarnation. It is not simply a birth which is celebrated at this time of year. The mystery of incarnation, the enfleshment of the Word of God in Jesus the Christ, is at the heart of this whole cycle. Both mystery and incarnation are crucial. At root the mystery of the incarnation is not simply a biological fact that can be subjected to objective and scientific scrutiny. It is a mystery which ultimately transcends any final and absolute grasp.

This is not to make light of the birth of Jesus of Nazareth in history. On the contrary, it is a reminder of the deep theological truths which are embodied in that birth. At Christmas Christians do not celebrate the birth of the best of all possible human beings in a primarily ethical sense. (From a traditional Catholic point of view such a claim can actually be made for Mary, mother of Jesus.) Christians celebrate Jesus as *Emmanuel*—"God with us." We make bold to claim that the mystery of God can be seen, heard and touched in Jesus Christ. God is everywhere, it is true; yet God is also somewhere —**here** in the person of Jesus. This is good news, indeed, and it has implications for any assertions which the Christian community makes about God's relationship to humanity, the world, and the whole cosmos.

The liturgy of this cycle reminds us that there is a "wonderful exchange" which has taken place. In one of the opening prayers (there are three possibilities) for the feast of the Baptism of the Lord, we pray that "we who share his (Christ's) divinity come to share his humanity." The Word has taken on our flesh and in so doing has divinized that flesh. Christ is our brother in the flesh; we are the offspring of God. There is deep mystery here and we can never finish plumbing its depth.

The incarnational dimension of this whole cycle also has implications for understanding the dynamics of Advent time. There is abroad the notion that Advent is a time to pretend that Christ has not yet come. However, this is not the spirit of Advent, nor is it found in its liturgical texts. For example, in the solemn blessing for the First Sunday of Advent we are reminded that we "believe that the Son of God once came to us" and we "look for him to come again." Christ has come, is coming, and will come again. Advent time reflects all of these comings. Liturgical remembrance is not a matter of pretense.

Mission-Oriented. The thrust of the Advent-Christmas-Epiphany cycle is one of outward movement in service to God's people and God's world. This is a dimension which is often overlooked. As individuals and as a community Christians can become so consumed with joyful waiting and/or in-house Christmas celebrations that they forget its essential outward mission thrust. It is not insignificant that the first words of the opening prayer at eucharist on the First Sunday of Advent pray that God might "increase our strength of will for doing good. . . ." This thrust continues to maintain itself throughout the whole cycle. For example, in the opening prayer for the dawn mass on Christmas Day we pray that the "light of faith shine in our words and actions." In the solemn blessing for the Baptism of the Lord the presider prays that the assembly "may continue to enjoy your (God's) favor and devote themselves to doing good." The liturgical texts at eucharist open and close this cycle with words of mission.

All this should give the church reason to pause and deeply reflect on its sense of mission, especially in light of Jesus' mission to the poor which is inaugurated in the incarnation. An often forgotten dimension of this cycle is the present advent/manifestation of God in Christ as God approaches us through the poor, suffering, marginalized and oppressed. Surely some time might be given to the exploration of that advent/manifestation in the liturgy. After all, the opening prayer for mass during the day on Christmas reminds us that Christ "shared our weakness. . . ." However, this is a delicate issue and must be dealt with in terms of the deepest dynamisms of the liturgical action. Particular social agendas, no matter how noble, should not be permitted to manipulate liturgy, but a proper Christian social consciousness is part of liturgical celebration during this cycle. (This is not to suggest that they never be admitted into the liturgy.) The liturgy is not education as we normally understand that term, nor is liturgical prayer to be confused with secular ideology. Liturgy is rooted in the praise of God and intercession on behalf of a sinful, broken world. It is neither a blatantly political nor economic rally. The Word became flesh in an oppressed land and in the condition of poverty, not at a political convention.

Emphases and Dynamisms. The Advent-Christmas-Epiphany cycle is best understood as one among several seasons of the church's year. It possesses its own special emphases and dynamisms. As has been noted elsewhere, the liturgical year is composed of various feasts and seasons. Though these share certain common denominators (for example, the paschal mystery) each possesses special emphases and dynamisms.

The key dynamism of the Advent-Christmas-Epiphany cycle can be said to be captured in the notion of **coming.** "Come" in its various forms continually appears in the liturgical prayer texts. For example, in the opening prayer for Monday of the first week of Advent we pray that we might be helped "to prepare for the coming of Christ." In the opening prayer for the mass at dawn on Christmas Day we acknowledge that we are a people "filled with new light by the coming of your (God's) Word among us." In the entrance anti-

phon for Epiphany we acclaim: "The Lord and ruler is coming."
Liturgically and theologically this whole cycle seeks to draw us into
the mystery of the coming and manifestation of God in Christ. This
coming and manifestation is celebrated in the historical events of
the incarnation and birth of Jesus, in the present ways in which God
in Christ comes to us and is manifested in our midst, and in the
tension of a future and ultimate manifestation and coming for
which the Christian community waits. Furthermore, other comings
and manifestations are celebrated during this cycle: the Annunciation, the Epiphany, and the Baptism of Jesus are among these. Thus,
it is inadequate to think of Advent as a time when we imagine we are
living in the past before the birth of the messiah. Likewise, Christmas is not simply the retelling of the events which surrounded the
birth of Jesus. Christmas is never simply a "birthday" celebration. It
commemorates the incarnation and birth of Jesus who came that we
might have new life in God through him.

There is a certain fluidity, even ambiguity, about all these
"comings" and manifestations. The liturgical celebrations of this
cycle remind us of the dynamisms of "incarnate coming"—that we
move in sacred time and sacred place and therefore we must keep
our eyes ever open and be ever watchful, for we know neither the
time(s) nor the place(s) of God's manifestation(s). While the incarnation and nativity of the Word remind us of God's concrete fidelity
to humanity, they also remind us that we must avoid a type of
imitative celebration which is simply a reiteration (or worse, repetition) of past events. Singing "happy birthday" to Jesus on Christmas
Day misses the point and eclipses the mystery of incarnation. It
tames Christmas and it tames God in Christ as well.

What is emerging here is the realization that the various comings and manifestations which are celebrated during this cycle are
not and should not be too easily nailed down, nor should they be too
readily separated. While each manifestation may have a special
focus, together they are bound up with one another.

Rank. Within the liturgical cycles the Advent-Christmas-Epiphany cycle is ranked as second in importance. It must first be remembered that the GNLYC speak about the "yearly cycle" and the cycle
of "liturgical days" (#3, 17). The central and primary celebration of
the whole liturgical year is always the paschal mystery. While this

mystery is at the heart of all the various feasts and seasons of the liturgical year, its fundamental and foundational celebration takes place during the Lent-Easter-Pentecost cycle, most especially during the celebration of the triduum (#18). Because of this the Lent-Easter-Pentecost cycle takes precedence in the yearly cycle.

In light of this observation regarding the layout of the GNLYC two important points must be recalled here. First, the layout suggests that the liturgical year is not to be considered simply as a series of celebrations remembering the chronological events in the life of Jesus of Nazareth. Second, the layout explicitly suggests that there is a hierarchy of importance in the various yearly and daily celebrations of the liturgical year. Some seasons and feasts are of greater or lesser importance than others. Furthermore, the seasons and feasts of lesser importance are celebrated in the light of those of greater importance. Specifically, the Advent-Christmas-Epiphany cycle is of secondary importance (though it is often treated popularly as being the most significant cycle in the liturgical year) (#32).

There are two related issues which can be raised at this point. It has become somewhat common to speak about Advent as the beginning of the liturgical year, yet the GNLYC never uses the term "beginning" in reference to Advent. There is no beginning or ending of the liturgical year in any strict or absolute sense. From a liturgical perspective it would be more accurate to speak about the liturgical year as composed of various cycles and days which flow one into another each year. It is difficult to pinpoint one beginning and one end. In one sense the notion of a "liturgical year" with a clearly marked beginning and ending is a kind of fictive construct.

If one feels compelled to employ this kind of language it would be better to speak about the liturgical year as having several different beginnings and endings, none of which can be too absolutely designated. For example, in many respects the First Sunday of Advent continues the eschatological themes of the preceding Sundays (the Thirty-second Sunday through the feast of Christ the King). There is actually a kind of merging of themes and images which takes place rather than some sort of "beginning" or "ending."

This is not to deny the need for some sense of beginning and closure in the celebration of the liturgical year. It is, however, a recognition that Advent need not be nailed down as the only possible place to celebrate the beginning of the liturgical year. As a matter of liturgical and theological reflection, it might be more accurate to understand the Advent-Christmas-Epiphany cycle as a time of closure, especially in light of its heavy eschatological overlay.

Specific mention must also be made here regarding the nature of the relationship between Advent and Christmas-Epiphany times. While the Advent-Christmas-Epiphany cycle ought to be considered as essentially a whole, not every dimension of the cycle is equally important. The GNLYC discusses Christmas before discussing Advent. This implies that Christmas time is of greater liturgical and theological significance than Advent time (#32–38). Advent is understood and celebrated in the shadow of Christmas. (It should be remembered that Advent is not common to all churches. Some eastern churches do not celebrate Advent as a distinct season.)

It was noted earlier that according to the GNLYC the thrust of Advent is a twofold preparation. It is a time of preparation for the celebration of God's presence among people in the incarnation of the Word, of which one dimension is the birth of Jesus. It is also a preparatory time geared toward reminding the Christian community that it yet awaits the second and ultimate coming of Christ at the consummation of history (#39).

Regarding the nature of this preparation there remains a question about the relationship between penance and Advent. While Christian life certainly involves penance, Advent is not to be understood as a special penitential season. It is not an imitation of Lent. (Remember that such a relationship seems to have arisen when the feast of Epiphany was celebrated as a time to baptize, baptism obviously involving a sense of conversion and penance.) Liturgically, the gospel "alleluia" continues to be sung during Advent (as opposed to its absence during Lent). It is true that the Gloria is not sung during Advent, but the *Commentary* on the GNLYC notes that the silencing of the Gloria during Advent is not a sign of penance but rather, that it might be sung with a certain newness and freshness on Christmas. The GNLYC notes that Advent is "a period for devout and joyful expectation" (#39). It makes no mention of penance.

These remarks concerning penance and Advent are not meant to discourage personal penances that any given individual might opt to undertake during Advent. Rather, they are meant to highlight that the liturgical time of Advent and the practice of penance are not essentially related.

At the same time this is not to deny that a certain austerity and simplification are appropriate to Advent. However, this austerity and simplification have more to do with clearing away the clutter of our lives that we might see more readily the approach and coming of God in Christ. Fasting, for example, need not be penitential. Optional fasting during Advent can be undertaken precisely as an attempt to unclutter our appetites.

Texts. The theology of the Advent-Christmas-Epiphany cycle is best unpacked when due consideration is given to its various liturgical texts. The importance of liturgical texts has been noted throughout this book. In unpacking the liturgical theology of this cycle (or of any given day within the cycle) it is best to consider and reflect on the liturgical texts themselves. Look for recurring words, images, ideas, personalities, and moods. Note how these interact with one another. For example, in working out a theology of the Advent-Christmas-Epiphany cycle the following ought not be ignored: light/darkness, Isaiah, John the Baptizer, Mary, waiting, coming, patience, promise, hope, peace, justice, judgment, baby, and so forth.

This is not to suggest that extra-textual and/or extra-liturgical dynamisms be ignored. It would be foolish to ignore celebrations, music, and customs associated with this time of year (for example, those associated with St. Nicholas and St. Lucy). In the section on pastoral issues a number of these will be discussed. These can be and are significant factors in the community's appropriation of this cycle. Furthermore, they have a role to play in working out a theology and spirituality for this cycle. However, it would be remiss for a community to celebrate this cycle without due attention to its liturgical texts. This is particularly pertinent to and important for the Advent-Christmas-Epiphany cycle, as this cycle is often understood through and interpreted by some crass commercial and materialistic practices, extra-liturgical carols, and ethnic and familial customs. The issue is not an either/or matter; rather, it is a both/and matter—both texts and contexts.

Tension/Balance. In working through the theology and spirituality of this cycle or any given day within it, a healthy tension and balance must be maintained between overgeneralization and over-specification. The paschal, eschatological and incarnational over-tones of this cycle have been noted. However, care must be taken not to overgeneralize the meaning of the cycle. This could lead to a lack of focus which would seriously compromise the cycle's ability to impact on the community and its liturgical celebrations. If the cycle means everything at every given liturgical celebration, it proba-bly means nothing at all. For example, the *Commentary* on the GNLYC notes that the period between the First Sunday of Advent and December 16 lends itself to consideration of the Second Com-ing of Christ. This is a legitimate focus during this period. It should be expressed, but with a certain fluidity. The difficulty arises when on the one hand this focus is ignored, or when on the other hand it is completely eclipsed once December 16 occurs and is "put away" until next Advent time. Likewise, on Christmas Day it is legitimate to focus on the incarnation of the Word in the birth of Jesus. How-ever, to let the birth of Jesus be the sole focus of this entire cycle (to the exclusion of the eschatological overtones as well as other mani-festations) is highly problematic liturgically and theologically.

This leads to one more caveat. Take care not to box the mean-ing of the cycle (or any particular day within it) into a corner. Allow for elasticity in the meaning and celebration of the cycle. If the Advent-Christmas-Epiphany cycle is allowed only one meaning it becomes impoverished and robbed of its power to evoke.

PASTORAL ISSUES AND CUSTOMS

Any liturgical team responsible for the shape of liturgical cele-brations during the Advent-Christmas-Epiphany cycle sooner or later begins to ask about concrete issues. What is the liturgical color of Advent time? Is it violet or blue? Should we place and use an Advent wreath in the church? Should we continue to use a crèche in church? Where should it be placed? Should we incorporate secular signs of the season into the liturgy? What should we sing? Is it appro-priate to sing Christmas songs in church prior to Christmas Day? When should we stop singing Christmas songs? And the list continues.

For some these issues might appear to be "fluffy" matters; however, it is actually dangerous to treat them as such. For better or worse, they factor greatly into individual and communal perceptions of this cycle. A spirituality and theology of the liturgical year cannot be adequately and properly addressed without considering these issues. As a matter of method it can be argued that these issues *must* be addressed as they are extremely formative of people's spirituality.

Color. The church has traditionally used violet as the Advent color. To many, however, violet tends to suggest penitential overtones. Violet is also the color of Lent, and in the realm of the imagination connections are made between Advent and Lent. Lent is a time imbued with certain penitential themes. Advent is not, and therein resides the problematic confusion between the spirit and overtones of these two times of the liturgical year. In pastoral practice three solutions have been offered to remedy this situation.

The *first solution* suggests the use of two different shades of violet, royal violet for Advent and penitential violet for Lent. It is thereby hoped that the two different shades of violet might convey the different spirits of these two times. In many respects, however, this appears to be a contrived distinction and probably does not yield the desired message to the community at large. Put crassly, "purple is purple" to most people and shades of purple do not seem to factor into perceptions. Furthermore, the two times of Advent and Lent are so removed from one another that the difference in shades of purple would probably not occur to many people.

The *second solution* employed by a growing number of parishes and communities is to use blue as the Advent color. As a seasonal liturgical color the use of blue is new to the Roman Catholic Church. Blue, however, has been used in the past in special vestments for celebrations in honor of Mary. The marian overtone of blue stands ironically as one of the real problems regarding its use. (The danger of this cycle being dominated by marian themes and celebrations has already been noted.) Advent is not a special marian season and any associations in this regard should be avoided. At the same time positive dimensions commend blue as the (or an) Advent color. First, it has ecumenical possibilities since it is now used by a number of Protestant communities as the Advent color. Second, it does help to move Advent time away from associations with Lent and Lenten penitence.

The *third solution* employed in some places involves a move toward the use of a combination of these colors. Such a combination serves to communicate the "tones" and "moods" of this time, that is, joyful waiting and anticipation. As such, a combination of the following colors might be suggested: shades of blue, violet, rose, gray, and light earthen tones. This allows for some continuity with the traditional Advent colors (violet and rose), the emergence of new Advent colors, and perhaps a more adequate capturing of the spirit of this time.

One caveat is in order. GIRM states that violet is the Advent color, and that the use of rose on the Third Sunday of Advent may be an option (#308). There is presently no law stating otherwise. Also, the use of blue is not, strictly speaking, a custom.

Before concluding these remarks on color a word is in order regarding the relationship of the theological and liturgical unity of the Advent-Christmas-Epiphany cycle, especially as this applies to the question of color. Should the basic unity of the cycle be expressed in the use of color? Perhaps the answer is both "no" and "yes." The different colors do indicate the varying foci which are part of this cycle. Thus, it is not necessary to use the same colors for the Christmas festival as were used for Advent time. Yet perhaps it might also be advisable to leave some vestiges of the Advent time colors present in the church during the Christmas festival and manifestation celebrations. This might help to convey the theological unity of the Advent-Christmas-Epiphany cycle as well as lessen the temptation toward an over-separation among the various celebrations of the cycle.

Advent Wreath. The Advent wreath has become a rather common sight in most churches during Advent time. It consists of four candles (sometimes three violet and one rose, sometimes four violet or blue) encircled by a wreath of evergreens. The candles are progressively lit with each passing week of Advent. There is sometimes a "Christ Candle" in the center of the wreath which is lighted during the Christmas festival.

The Advent wreath originated among German Lutherans in the sixteenth century. It gained popularity among both Protestants and Catholics and was brought to the United States by German immigrants. It originated in the home but was soon imported into the churches. Today it is a custom in both homes and churches.

There is a certain polyvalence about its symbolism. Some have suggested that its essential symbolism consists in the circle of evergreens. Others suggest that its essential symbolism is rooted in the light of its flames. This sort of talk is deadly to a proper notion of symbolism. The wreath is symbolic in many ways. It is, however, interesting to note that various prayers for the blessing of the wreath tend to concentrate on the light symbolism. For example, the prayer for the blessing of the Advent wreath contained in the ***Book of Blessings*** prays that "as we light the candles of this wreath; may their light reflect the splendor of Christ. . . ." Likewise, the prayer for the blessing of an Advent wreath contained in the ***Catholic Household Blessings and Prayers*** prays that the "wreath and its light" may be "a sign of Christ's promise to bring us salvation." In neither book is there any mention of evergreens. Again, in ***A Book of Blessings*** published by the Canadian bishops, the prayer asks that the wreath might be "a sign of his (Christ's) light among us." There is, again, no mention of evergreens.

There are a number of resources available which offer possibilities for the place of the wreath in home settings. The concern here has to do with the incorporation of the wreath into a liturgical setting. These are offered by way of cautions.

1. The wreath needs to be blessed only once and at one liturgy. There is the practice in some parishes of a blessing prayer at every liturgy and on every Sunday of Advent. This is unnecessarily redundant. Those who plan such a liturgy should consult the ***Book of Blessings,*** pp. 647–657.

2. The wreath should be constructed in such a way that it is capable of functioning as a public symbol. It should be noble, beautiful, sturdy and of adequate size. A tiny home wreath on a small table next to the altar will not do. Most liturgists suggest a sizable wreath suspended from the ceiling (see ***Book of Blessings,*** para. 1512).

3. The wreath should not be located in such a way that it competes with or overshadows more dominant liturgical symbols (for example, the altar, see ***Book of Blessings,*** para. 1512).

4. When the wreath is blessed at the beginning of Advent and

as each candle is progressively lit, the prayer texts should focus on the "light" symbolism rather than the "evergreen" or "circular" symbolism. Such "light" symbolism lends itself more readily to the other scriptural and liturgical symbols of Advent time.

5. The blessing and lighting prayer is best done at the evening liturgy, especially as this is a time of darkness in most places in the northern hemisphere (see *Book of Blessings,* para. 1509, 1513).

Christmas Crèche. It is common practice in many parish churches, religious communities, and homes to set up a Christmas crèche. The practice is often traced back to St. Francis of Assisi who was noted for setting up a "living" nativity scene. Once again, this practice cannot be ignored here because it is so central to the Christmas rituals of many people. For many, it is "the" religious symbol of this time of the year. For better or worse it also finds its way into the liturgy either through some direct liturgical incorporation or by some more subtle practice (such as its placement in proximity to the altar, and so forth). There is no pressing reason why such practices should not be continued, but there are some clarifications which must be made.

The basic problem with the crèche is that it tends to draw attention to only one dimension of the Advent-Christmas-Epiphany cycle, that is, the birth of Jesus in Bethlehem. This is certainly a legitimate focus but it must be complemented by others as well. This is particularly crucial when the crèche is exhibited in a parish church or public chapel. Practices such as setting up the crèche prior to Christmas while leaving the manger empty until Christmas Eve or Day can be liturgically and theologically problematic. The use of the crèche is not a liturgical practice per se. It belongs to the realm of extra-liturgical popular practice. In many subtle ways the crèche can and does become the focus of much energy during this cycle. For example, practices such as making a manger from straws representing good deeds and visitation of families to the manger yield that this is so. Such focusing must sometimes be circumscribed liturgically. The crèche is at the service of the liturgy, not vice versa. The presence of the crèche must not be allowed to kidnap the meaning of this cycle. Thus, some sort of catechesis should probably accompany the use of the crèche.

In addition to catechesis about the crèche it might be worthwhile for a community to entertain the possibility of other visual art forms which might draw attention to other dimensions of the Advent-Christmas-Epiphany cycle. An interesting example of such an art form is the "Etimasia." The "Etimasia" is the empty throne of the Pantocrator which can be found in a number of early mosaics. The thrust of the image is clearly eschatological and it might serve nicely to complement the incarnational accent of the crèche.

It might also be a welcome change to explore other possible ways to visually represent the nativity. The use of an icon (for example, of Mary holding Jesus or the Pantocrator) is one such possibility.

The abolition of the crèche is certainly not being advocated here. The use of the crèche alone, however, is purposely questioned. Francis of Assisi used his nativity scene to bring the radical poverty and humility of the incarnation into focus. The prayer contained in the **Book of Blessings** for blessing the manger during mass is instructive on this point: ". . . may it (the manger) remind us of the humble birth of Jesus, and raise up our thoughts to him, who is God-with-us and Savior of all. . . ." Unfortunately some of our commercialized nativity scenes do not do that.

The following suggestions might be considered:

1. Do not display the crèche in home or church prior to the Third Sunday of Advent. Allow the first two weeks of Advent to highlight the eschatological overtones of this cycle.

2. Give some consideration to the absence/presence of the statue of the infant in the manger. In many places it is customary to set up the crèche prior to Christmas Eve while leaving the manger empty. This can become problematic in that it tends to overemphasize the past event to the detriment of the existential and eschatological dimensions. Generally such an action (for example, having a member of the assembly place the statue of the infant in the manger during the reading of the gospel at midnight mass) should not be incorporated into the liturgy. Perhaps the easiest solution is to wait until Christmas Eve to set up the crèche.

3. The crèche should not compete with central liturgical symbols or crucial liturgical furnishings. The presider's chair and the place for the proclamation of the scriptures should be respected. The

central place of the altar should never be usurped. (The altar should not serve as a sort of "cave" or "barn" with the crèche displayed at its base. Remember: the altar itself is "the symbol" of Christ within the assembly.) Generally speaking, the crèche is best placed at some distance from altar/ambo/chair where it can be seen and visited by the assembly, yet does not become the focus of the assembly's liturgical celebration. The ***Book of Blessings*** clearly states that "If the manger is set up in the church, it must not be placed in the presbyterium" (para. 1544). When all is said and done, remember that essentially God in Christ comes to birth in the assembly, not in objects crafted for a crèche.

Scents. In many parishes and communities certain scents (for example, pine) are associated with this time of year. There is no pressing reason why the liturgical assembly ought not capitalize on these. We worship with our whole being, including our noses.

Christmas Tree. The Christmas tree has become a common sight in many homes. However, its use in church is also becoming popular. The ***Book of Blessings*** now contains an "Order for the Blessing of a Christmas Tree." This is hardly surprising. The Catholic church, with its rather positive outlook on creation, has always been rather liberal in its blessing of things.

Two points, however, are in order here. First, the texts of the blessing tend to emphasize the lighted and decorated tree as a symbol of the light and joy of Christ. Second, the Christmas tree does possess liturgical and catechetical potential for making connections between the incarnation and Christ's Pasch. For example, the second optional prayer of blessing notes that the cross has been made a "tree of life and light." Furthermore, the blessing continues by praying that this tree may "remind us of the life-giving cross of Christ. . . ." The community should capitalize on these connections.

Music. The selection and use of appropriate liturgical music for the Advent-Christmas-Epiphany cycle tends to be a confused and complex matter at times. Catechumens, lifetime Catholics, and liturgical planners are often bewildered by what is sung and what is not sung during this cycle. The various foci within this cycle demand different moods and texts at different times. Hymn, carol, and song texts are particularly crucial. They mark this time as being different and they convey a theology of the cycle that is often experientially more powerful and memorable than liturgical prayer texts. This section will seek to clarify some matters.

Texts—The theological and liturgical foci of this cycle are essentially related but not always interchangeable. For this reason attention must be paid to the texts of songs. Every song contained in the Advent section of the parish hymnal is not necessarily appropriate for every and any day of Advent time. This is likewise true about Christmas songs as well as songs which celebrate the various manifestation feasts. This is not to deny, however, that there may be some songs which lend themselves to two or more of the foci of this cycle (for example, Lucien Deiss' "Zion Sing"). Regarding song texts for this cycle, consider the following:

1) The opening weeks of Advent highlight eschatological hopes associated with the Second Coming. These weeks are not a time to concentrate on "waiting" for the birth of the "babe of Bethlehem." Texts which look forward primarily to the birth of Jesus on Christmas Day are here thus inappropriate. Rather, texts should express the dynamisms and images that are associated with the Christ's return in glory. Consider the text of "Come, Lord, and Tarry Not":

> Come, Lord, and tarry not!
> Bring the long looked-for day!
> Oh, why these years of waiting here,
> These ages of delay?
>
> Come, for your saints still wait;
> Daily ascends their sigh;
> The Spirit and the Bride say, "Come!"
> Do you not hear the cry?
>
> Come, for creation longs,
> Impatient of delay,
> And yearns for endless years of good,
> Bright ages of your stay.

Come, and make all things new,
Come, save this longing earth;
Transform all creatures in your love,
Creation's second birth.

Come, and begin your reign,
Of everlasting peace;
Come, take the kingdom to yourself
Great King of righteousness!

Notice the text, its images and mood. Its tone is one of intense longing and yearning. The image is not one of "birth" but one of "coming." The text reminds us that we wait not for the birth of a baby but rather for the coming of an adult Lord. The use of the word "Lord" here is packed with eschatological content. Coming, warning, glory, judgment, Christ—these are the images and stuff of eschatology and they are the stuff of the opening weeks of Advent (as well as the weeks immediately prior to Advent).

2) The days immediately prior to Christmas (December 17 to December 24) look toward the liturgical commemoration of the birth of Jesus. The songs of these days ought to reflect this shift of emphasis. This is not to suggest that songs with eschatological thrusts should be totally eclipsed. However, the texts of some songs should reflect the shift. Also, this is not a green light for the singing of strictly Christmas songs. Most Christmas songs are appropriately reserved for the Christmas festival.

There are a number of Advent songs which express wonderfully a tension between the celebration of Jesus' birth and the Second Coming of Christ. "O Come, Divine Messiah" is such a song:

O come, Divine Messiah;
The world in silence waits the day
When hope shall sing its triumph
And sadness flee away

Refrain: Dear Savior, haste! Come, come to earth.
Dispel the night and show your face,
And bid us hail the dawn of grace.

O come, Divine Messiah;
The world in silence waits the day
When hope shall sing its triumph
And sadness flee away.

O Christ, whom nations sighed for,
Whom priest and prophet long foretold,
Come, break the captives' fetters,
Redeem the long lost fold.

Refrain

You come in peace and meekness
And lowly will your cradle be;
All clothed in human weakness
Shall we your Godhead see.

Refrain

Notice the tension which is present in this text. On the one hand there are clear eschatological overtones. On the other hand the birth of Jesus is also noted.

3) Part of the built-in problem here is the presentation of Advent songs in many hymnals. There is often no differentiation between those songs which are most appropriate for the opening weeks of Advent and those which are appropriate to its final days. Liturgically, however, texts ought to reflect the difference. In choosing appropriate Advent songs it is most helpful to consult and reflect on the entrance and communion antiphons of the given day. These antiphons (as has been noted elsewhere) often convey the theological and liturgical overtones which mark the day's liturgy.

A consideration of the images contained in the various songs is often a helpful way to determine the time during Advent when a particular song may be appropriate. For example, Advent songs with concrete Christmas images (for example, birth, baby, Mary, manger, and so forth) are appropriate to the days immediately prior to Christmas. The Liturgy of the Hours suggests that the "O Antiphons" are appropriate to the days before Christmas. Thus, the final two Sundays (as well as December 17 onward) are certainly good times to use the traditional "O Come, O Come Emmanuel."

4) Two caveats are in order. First, Advent is not a time to dwell exclusively and excessively on certain Advent personalities. Isaiah, John the Baptizer, and Mary should not be dwelt on in isolated fashion. Second, the brand of eschatology which is proclaimed during Advent should be examined. Advent is not meant to be a four-week reflection on a person's individual death and judgment. But this is not to imply that mention of these realities should be completely avoided. The texts of the sacramentary and lectionary, however, do tend toward a ***corporate eschatology*** as the focus of the opening weeks of Advent. As a community we await the coming of Christ in glory.

5) An examination of the Christmas section of any hymnal reveals that the Christian community has a large repertoire of Christmas music at its disposal. Those who prepare the community's Christmas festival liturgies should make use of the variety which exists. The community, however, should not be bombarded by an endless variety. It might be wise to choose a core of songs which will be used as the community's musical staple during this time. (Of course, the frequency with which any given community gathers to celebrate eucharist, hours, and so forth, will determine the size and content of this repertoire.)

The teaching and learning of new songs at this time should be carefully considered. The Christmas festival is not long and the number of Christmas songs is already quite large. However, when new songs are considered, attention should be given to texts and music which have something fresh and insightful to say about the mysteries celebrated during this cycle.

6) Secular mass media tends to stop playing Christmas songs immediately after Christmas day. This practice is much connected with the commercialism of the season. The secular mass media now looks forward to the next commercial holiday. Liturgy ought not to imitate this practice. There is, however, a certain legitimacy to the question: How long should Christmas songs be sung in church? The shape of the answer is directly related to the particular Christmas song which is under consideration. Christmas songs are certainly sung throughout the Christmas festival (the octave). Once the festi-

val is over, however, it is advisable to set aside those songs which employ images of the birth of Jesus (manger, hay, angels' songs, and so forth). To continue to employ these songs is to run the risk of overemphasizing this one dimension of the cycle while eclipsing the "manifestation" feasts. Songs which deal with the general theological dynamisms of this time (for example, the enfleshment of the Word) should continue in use. Songs which celebrate the various "manifestation" feasts should also come to the fore. (In this regard it is interesting to note that certain hymnals now specify an "Epiphany" section and/or a "Baptism of the Lord" section containing songs which more properly belong to the manifestation feasts.)

Mood—There is an Advent mood and Christmas mood which is difficult to describe. The community knows it by experience. Be sensitive to those moods, especially by way of music. The mood of Advent music is generally different from the mood of Christmas festival music.

Religious—It should be fairly obvious that liturgical music be always theologically and religiously informed. God in Jesus Christ, not Santa, "coming to town," is the expected One. Generally speaking, seasonal songs with exclusively secular lyrics and images ought to be absent from Christian liturgy. White Christmases, jingle bells, happy birthdays, and Rudolf do not belong in Christian liturgy, not even children's liturgy.

Tradition—Christmas is a time packed with tradition. Many communities associate the various times and celebrations of this cycle with the singing of particular songs. Those planning the liturgies should not offend the community and jeopardize its liturgical celebrations by overlooking these traditions (unless, of course, they are anti-liturgical, un-theological, and/or ideologically distorted). For example, to celebrate Christmas Eve liturgy in a traditional parish using only recent and "trendy" Christmas compositions is at best foolhardy, and at worst arrogant.

Liturgy of the Hours/Community Prayer. In many places there has been catechesis regarding the Liturgy of the Hours and many people pray the Hours individually and/or communally. Many more, however, are the parishes and communities where this is not happening. The Advent-Christmas-Epiphany cycle is an opportune time for a parish to consider praying the Hours communally. Those parishes which have priests and/or religious (obviously not all do) might find in them a source of encouragement and help in initiating the Hours in a parish community context. The remarks made here presume a community context in which the arrangements of time, place, ministries, and format have been worked out. One further presumption is that the volume called **Christian Prayer** serves as a model for developing the Hours in a parish setting.

1) There is an immense body of non-scriptural religious poetry and prose which focuses on this cycle. Where possible some consideration might be given to incorporating this literature into the Liturgy of the Hours or other communal prayer forms. See, for example, Liturgy Training Publication's **An Advent Sourcebook,** and **A Christmas Sourcebook.**

2) In order to lend greater continuity to the Liturgy of the Hours it might be helpful to select one or two prophetic books of the Hebrew scriptures to be read throughout the whole cycle. This might also help to foster a "listening" posture rather than a "reading" posture in those communities where books are available. Similarly it might also be a good idea to use one or two scriptural responses related to the foci of this cycle. This response should be brief, sung, simple, and tasteful.

3) As was mentioned earlier, this cycle is a good time to entertain the possibility of using scents and/or incense. Evening prayer certainly lends itself to the use of incense. The swinging of thuribles is not being envisioned here. Rather, perhaps a bowl of incense could be burned in the center of the assembly, before an icon, or before the reserved holy bread.

4) In much of the northern western hemisphere the whole winter solstice celebration is built on the dynamics of light and darkness. Within the context of the Liturgy of the Hours, evening prayer might be a good time to employ this imagery. One possible suggestion: a simplified form of evening prayer in which as little light as possible is needed.

For Personal Reflection and/or Group Discussion

1. Do you experience your parish/community as one which is attuned to the Second Coming of Christ? How does the parish/community celebrate Advent? As a preparation for the Second Coming? As a preparation for Christmas?

2. Read and study the *prefaces* (P–1 through P–7) for the Advent-Christmas-Epiphany cycle. What (if any) is the eschatological thrust of each preface? How are the two Advent prefaces similar to each other? Different from each other? How is the eschatological thrust of the Advent prefaces similar to or different from that of the other prefaces of this season?

3. Examine the opening prayer at eucharist for the Christmas vigil mass, mass at midnight, mass at dawn, mass during the day. What words, images, and metaphors are used to describe the feast?

4. Do you think that the Christian community thinks of the Christmas celebration in terms of "birth" or "incarnation"?

5. The feast of the "Holy Innocents" is one which is often overlooked by large segments of the parish; yet it is also a feast which could be creatively reappropriated. There continue to be "holy innocents" who even now die unmourned and unsung. These "holy innocents" rest in anonymous and unknown tombs. Look at the texts for this feast in the sacramentary and lectionary. How might this feast be celebrated so that large numbers of people in the parish could remember and pray for the victims of history—the poor, the aborted, the forgotten elderly, the abused, people with AIDS, and . . . ?

7

The Sanctoral Cycle

In his holy flirtation with the world, God occasionally drops a handkerchief. These handkerchiefs are called saints.

FREDERICK BUECHNER, *WISHFUL THINKING*

. . . the effect of her being on those around her was incalculably diffusive: for the growing good of the world is partly dependent on unhistoric acts; and that things are not so ill with you and me as they might have been, is half owing to the number who lived faithfully a hidden life, and rest in unvisited tombs.

GEORGE ELLIOT, *MIDDLEMARCH*

HISTORICAL BACKGROUND

The development of a "cult of the martyrs" by the early Roman Christians must be understood against the backdrop of the eschatological beliefs of those Christians as well as the general cult of the dead as practiced in Rome and its environs.

In the New Testament one finds a certain tension between what have come to be differentiated as "realized" and "futurist" eschatologies. "Realized" eschatology tends to emphasize the completeness and present reality of the salvation won by Christ's life, death and resurrection. Its focus emphasizes that even now we are living in the "eschaton," the new and final age which was ushered in by the coming of Jesus the Christ. "Futurist" eschatology, on the other hand, tends to emphasize the belief that there is more yet to come—the Second Coming, the resurrection of the dead, the judgment, and the end of the world. The eschaton remains incomplete and "up ahead." The various components of this future eschaton were generally understood to be **corporate** realities, that is, realities that the community would experience communally rather than individually. The "judgment," for example, was a future corporate reality. This judgment would be experienced by the community (certainly in a personal way) rather than by individuals in a privatized fashion. The first generations of Christians evidently did not think in the aggressively individualistic categories that came to mark later generations. It was only with time and a delayed Second Coming that the notion of a privatized judgment began to appear.

These New Testament eschatological beliefs fused with certain Roman practices associated with the cult of the dead. The first practice which was assimilated was the general honor paid to the bodies of the dead. The second had to do with funeral meals that were celebrated at the tombs of the dead on their birthdays. This assimilation, however, was not simply a matter of carrying over popular practices, but involved a shift in practice and understanding. These practices were slowly transformed by the early Christian community in Rome to yield a cult of veneration in honor of the martyrs.

Some of these shifts are not to be overlooked because they have yielded many of the present practices still used as part of the Catholic veneration of the saints. First, the cult of the martyrs as practiced by the Roman Christians was different from the typical Roman cult of the dead in that it involved an acknowledgment of the martyr by the general community (rather than simply "relatives"). Keeping memory of the martyrs was not simply a family matter, but a community matter. Second, the martyrs were honored on the day of their death rather than their birthday. The early Roman Christians considered the day of martyrdom to be the true birth of the martyr, a birth into paradise by the witness of giving up life itself for the sake of Christ. The early Roman Christians also believed that the martyrs possessed great intercessory power. Roman Christians would often call out to those who were being led to martyrdom in the hope that after death these martyrs would remember those on earth. Today one can still find ancient intercessory "graffiti" scratched on the tombs of martyrs.

The eventual historical and theological development of the cult of the saints was a somewhat complex process, and time and space do not permit an exhaustive analysis. Three general historical dynamisms, however, will be noted here.

First, with time there was a shift from a cult of the martyrs to a cult that included other holy dead as well. At first only the martyrs were venerated. For example, there is evidence that as early as 155 C.E. Polycarp was venerated in Asia Minor. The earliest evidence of such veneration in the west comes from North Africa circa 180 C.E. There is no evidence of such veneration in Rome until the third century. Eventually, however, the practice of such veneration was extended to many Christian communities. "Confessors" (those who were imprisoned and/or suffered but were not killed) also came to be included among the venerated as well. With the closing of the period of persecutions still other "saints" were included—among whom were ascetics, virgins, and bishops.

Second, there was a gradual shift from a local sanctoral calendar to one that was more universal in scope. Initially the sanctoral calendar was characterized by its particularity, through which the memory of local martyrs and saints was celebrated. Though the memory of some saints was celebrated throughout several regions, even these began in particular local churches. The determination of which saints to commemorate resided with the local bishop. A certain precedence was given to commemorations of early martyrs and saints. By the eleventh and twelfth centuries, and with the emergence of conflicts regarding certain sanctoral celebrations, some bishops started to appeal to the authority of Rome to regulate the matter. This set the stage for the centralization and universalization of sanctoral celebrations. (The canonization process as we know it, however, did not come into being until the fifteenth century.)

There is an important point here which should not be underestimated. There existed a certain existential relationship between martyrs and saints and the other faithful. The martyrs and saints initially were people who had been well-known by the community. Thus, the cult of the martyrs and saints was a "popular" as well as a "from the bottom-up" movement. The bonds of solidarity between the dead martyrs and saints had been forged in existential relationships in actual life together in Christian community.

The final historical dynamism to be noted here was (and is) the tendency to move from a less to a more populated sanctoral calendar. Eventually the liturgical year became quite cluttered with sanctoral celebrations, which have persisted since the twelfth century. For example, one of the reforms of the Tridentine calendar was the reduction of the number of sanctoral celebrations from approximately 300 to 150. While the reform of the liturgical calendar initiated by the Second Vatican Council did much to simplify the sanctoral calendar, we continue to live with sanctoral clutter in the calendar. A simplification in the system of liturgical ranking as well as a reduction of the number of sanctoral days has helped the emergence of more theologically and liturgically crucial celebrations. Since the initial post-conciliar reforms, however, a number of sanctoral celebrations (both universal and particular) have emerged. The present challenge is to beware of a creeping tendency to once again clutter the sanctoral calendar.

GENERAL PRINCIPLES

Graced. When we honor the saints we are effectively praising the grace of God which has triumphed in their lives. Christianity is not simply the political, economic, societal transformation and/or renovation of the world, nor is it exclusively the embodiment of God's grace within the "structures" of society. Rather, Christianity involves the proclamation of God's unconditional love, mercy and justice for us in Christ, especially as these lay hold of the lives of concrete human beings. From this perspective it is possible to understand the human person as possessing the capacity to be a kind of "epiphany" of God, a disclosure of the divine.

The Catholic church has traditionally honored persons whose lives have intensely and publicly reflected God's love in Christ. This honor must be understood within a broader christological, ecclesiological, and anthropological context. When the church honors a saint it is actually praising the grace of God which has triumphed in the saint's life. The first movement is always on God's part. The various liturgical prayers of the sanctoral cycle indicate this clearly. For example, in the opening prayer for the liturgical memorial in honor of Philip Neri (May 26) the community addresses God as "you [who] continually raise up your faithful to the glory of holiness."

Within the context of both liturgy and devotion the honor which is given to saints is in no way meant as an affront to the central place of Christ. Rather, while we speak about Jesus Christ as the one mediator, it is possible from a Catholic perspective to speak about many and varied mediations. While salvation is personal, it is never privatistic or isolated. We are saved in and as community. Salvation's infrastructure is one of solidarity. Jesus Christ is never simply *my* personal savior; rather, he is *our* personal savior.

In general the liturgical year and its celebrations are especially attuned to these dynamics, for the liturgical year is the continual commemoration of the saving life, death and resurrection of the One who calls us into a community of grace.

Public. The saints are placed before the ecclesial community as public witnesses to, and concrete examples of, living the Christian vision. By public witness the saints function to challenge the Christian community. They embody the "dangerous memory of Jesus Christ" and confront the Christian community with the demands made by that memory on the individual's and community's own public witness. As such, remembering and honoring the saints is a prophetic dimension of the church's inner life. While one can derive a certain comfort from contemplating the solidarity which the saints in glory share with the pilgrim saints on earth, that comfort should not lead to a settled coziness.

Here one must recall the centrality of the paschal mystery in the liturgical year. The sanctoral celebrations are also celebrations of that mystery. This is particularly evident in martyrial celebrations and is often expressed through the image and symbol of **blood.** For example, on the liturgical memorial in honor of Charles Lwanga and companions (June 3) we pray, "Father, you have made the blood of the martyrs the seed of Christians." On the feast of Boniface (June 5) we pray, "Lord, your martyr Boniface spread the faith by his teaching and witnessed it with his blood." At the liturgy in honor of the first martyrs of Rome (June 30) we pray, "Father, you sanctified the Church of Rome with the blood of its first martyrs."

In their concrete lives the saints were and continue to be witnesses to the life, death and resurrection of Jesus Christ. The saints, thus, are *paschal witnesses.* The sanctoral celebrations of the liturgical year bring to the center of the ecclesial community's memory real persons who witnessed to the place of Jesus' life, death and resurrection in their lives.

The saints in their concrete lives also stand as reminders of the many different and legitimate ways in which God's grace can be embodied and by which witness to the paschal mystery can be given. "They inspire us by their heroic lives" (Preface II, Holy Men and Women). It must be remembered that this heroic Christian holiness takes many shapes that vary from person to person, place to place, and time to time. A Thomas Aquinas and a Louise de Marillac are rather different but legitimate witnesses to the power of God's grace in Christ.

Dynamics. The veneration of saints as expressed and celebrated in the church's cycle of seasons and feasts involves a twofold dynamic. First, the memory of the saint is placed before the community. Second, the dynamic of *intercession* is employed. In the sanctoral celebrations of the liturgical year the concrete life of the saint(s) is remembered by the praying church. The opening prayer of the eucharistic liturgy for the various sanctoral celebrations will often mention some specific quality or deed of the particular saint's life. For example, in the opening prayer for the memorial of St. Anthony of Padua (June 13) the community prays: "Almighty God, you have given St. Anthony to your people as an outstanding preacher. . . ." Likewise, the opening prayer for the memorial of St. Frances Xavier Cabrini (November 13) prays: "God our Father, you called Frances Xavier Cabrini from Italy to serve the immigrants of America." This quality of biographical concreteness is important precisely because it manifests the flesh and blood triumph of God's grace. The sanctoral celebrations remember real people rather than fantasies and semi-mythical creatures. However, this is not to deny the role and value of the legendary dimensions of hagiography.

The praying church, however, does not simply recall the past events of a saint's life in its sanctoral celebrations. In the liturgical prayers of both eucharist and hours there is often mention of the saint's intercession. In the opening prayer for the feast of St. Blase (February 3), for example, we pray: "Lord, hear the prayer of your martyr Blaise." On the feast of Sts. Perpetua and Felicity (March 7) we pray: "By their prayers, help us to grow in love of you [God]."

By this dynamic of "intercession" the church affirms the belief and hope that the saints are alive in God even now and that the saints in glory continue to be in solidarity with the pilgrim saints on earth. This image of "intercession" as a form of solidarity is an important one for the reappropriation of intercessory prayer today. It might be more helpful today to understand the dynamic of "intercession" as "being with" rather than "being between" or "being in place of." It is predicated on a broad and rather traditional understanding of the *communion of saints.*

This is not to suggest, however, that the saints are generally invoked in any direct fashion in liturgy. The liturgy is rather sparing in terms of any direct invocation of saints. One finds such direct invocation in the "Litany of Saints" used at the Easter vigil, at ordination ceremonies, and at baptisms. One also finds it in the "**A**" form of the penitential rite used at eucharist. Other than these and a few other times the saints are not invoked directly in liturgical assemblies. Such direct invocation generally belongs to personal and communal popular devotion forms. The opening prayer as well as various other presidential prayers of the sanctoral celebrations will often mention the name and intercession of the saint being remembered, *but these prayers are addressed directly to God.*

The saints who are honored in the liturgy are those who have been officially recognized as such by ecclesial authorities. The usual process for this in our own day is beatification and canonization. Due to the financial, political, and ideological factors often at work in this process, much criticism has been registered regarding it. Certainly there is validity to these criticisms. In light of this some local communities are eager to incorporate more contemporary uncanonized saints into liturgical celebrations. In many places this is already being done. This is understandable but caution is also in order with regard to this practice. Sometimes time and a more universal vision can help a community in the process of discerning what holiness is and in whom it is publicly witnessed.

There is both a general and particular calendar of saints. More will be said about this distinction later in the chapter.

Variety. In the Catholic tradition the veneration of saints has been and can be expressed in a variety of ways. Liturgy is but one way. In addition to liturgy both personal and communal devotions have been and are used to honor the saints. In recent times the "novena" has been one of the more familiar communal forms of such devotion.

In this regard the relationship between liturgy and communal devotions is one which is in need of some reconsideration. On the one hand a legitimate distinction between the two is certainly needed. The two should generally not be confused and steps should be taken to insure that in some instances a clear distinction is maintained. For example, on the practical level questions should be raised regarding the incorporation of novena prayers into the framework of the eucharist or Liturgy of the Hours. On the other hand, the relationship between devotions and liturgy (if any) needs to be explored. Questions must continue to be raised. What is the theological differentiation between the "devotion" and the "liturgy"? Is legitimation by certain ecclesial authorities the determining factor in this distinction?

In a similar vein the cult of the saints cannot be said to be limited simply to those who are named in official universal and/or particular calendars. There exists a plethora of other saints as well (including the unknown and unnamed who have been lost and forgotten by history). How best to remember and celebrate some of these saints remains a question for ecclesial communities.

Many people also continue to maintain a *personal calendar* of saints. The memory and celebration of dead relatives looms large here. With regard to these saints and the ways in which they are remembered two points are in order. First, there must be some sensitivity to their presence. Second, there must be some positive criticism as well as a search for ways to remember them communally. In the past the liturgy of "All Souls" as well as prayers for the "poor souls" were expressions of such sensitivity. However, we are in need of new and creative ways to be in solidarity as a pilgrim community with our relatives and friends who have died into the mystery of God.

Finally, it should always and everywhere be recalled that the saints are best honored by a cult of imitation of Christ—lives of discipleship in which dying and rising with Jesus the Christ is evidenced.

PRINCIPLES OF REFORM

The most recent reforms of the sanctoral cycle have already been noted. A number of clear principles were operative in these reforms and it is helpful to note these principles here. Before considering these, however, two basic insights must be noted. First, these basic principles are undergirded by theological and liturgical presuppositions, which will emerge more clearly as the individual principles are examined. Second, these principles should impact on pastoral decisions regarding the concrete shape that various sanctoral celebrations take in any given context.

Hierarchy. The seasonal cycles of the liturgical year take precedence over the sanctoral cycle. Generally speaking, Sundays, feasts of the Lord, and the various liturgical seasons are more central in the liturgical year than the various individual sanctoral celebrations. This is not to imply that one may dismiss sanctoral celebrations on a whim or that such celebrations may be eliminated entirely. As a whole the individual sanctoral celebrations are known as the sanctoral cycle. They are placed in their own unique section known as the "Proper of the Saints" in the sacramentary. However, the various celebrations in honor of the saints must be contextualized and understood within the broader and more important cycles and celebrations of the liturgical year. For example, appropriate contextualization may be expressed at times in a decision to suspend certain optional memorials in order to allow the more central dynamisms of a particular cycle to emerge. Advent and Lent ought not be cluttered with individual sanctoral celebrations. Where it is impossible to suspend such celebrations because of law or culture those who have the responsibility for preparing and leading the community's worship might consider how the individual sanctoral celebrations can best be appropriated into the dynamisms of the particular cycle.

Sound theological, liturgical and pastoral criteria need to be developed for and applied to decisions regarding the liturgical celebration (or absence thereof) of individual saints. Among the questions which might be asked are the following: 1) Is the saint truly significant to and for this particular community? 2) Is there some prophetic dimension of the saint's life and message which needs to be heard by this community? 3) Does liturgical law allow for the suspension of this particular sanctoral celebration? 4) Can the celebration of this particular saint be properly contextualized within the Advent-Christmas-Epiphany cycle or the Lent-Easter-Pentecost cycle?

Idea Feasts. The number of "idea" celebrations, i.e., those which have more to do with the promotion of certain "ideas," should be limited. A number of celebrations in the former liturgical calendar as well as the reformed calendar have their origins in a concern to propagate certain "ideas." For example, the feast of St. Joseph the Worker (May 1) originated in reaction to May Day celebrations which were socialist in overtone. Likewise, the feast of the Holy Family (Sunday within the octave of Christmas) was highlighted in order to protect and emphasize the important place of the family in the Christian lifestyle. The promotion of certain "ideologies" can be, of course, somewhat questionable and sometimes dangerous.

In a sense this principle bodes well for the celebrations of the sanctoral cycle. These celebrations are generally rooted in the memory of concrete lives of particular individuals. This principle also helps to focus some guidelines regarding the "content" of sanctoral celebrations. These celebrations ought not become battlegrounds for competing ideologies. The Christian community needs other forums for such ideological undertakings.

History. Saints who are honored liturgically ought to be rooted in history. There ought to be some firm basis in history for the life of any saint who is honored liturgically. Thus, it would seem important that there be greater knowledge about the saint than merely his or her name and the date of martyrdom/death. It has already been noted that Christianity is something more than simply a collection of fine ideas. By the same token the celebration of Christian witness via liturgical sanctoral celebrations should not be reduced to a collection of pious legends about persons whose historicity is questionable.

In this matter, however, some sensitivity must be exercised. The elimination or absence of a saint from the liturgical calendar is not necessarily going to signal the absence of the saint from people's lives (nor should it necessarily). For example, consider St. Christopher and the legend associated with him. Parishes remain which have been named in his honor. His figure continues to decorate the dashboards of cars, boats and planes. His medal continues to be worn. Recently a new contemporized icon of St. Christopher has appeared on the market. The legend of St. Christopher reflects the significance of popular religion and popular religious customs. One must be careful about too readily debunking it. The basic concern here is not to debunk legendary saints who have factored into peoples lives powerfully, but rather to question the propriety of celebrating the memory of such saints liturgically. Generally speaking, it seems best not to construct and/or maintain a liturgical cult around such figures, though certain circumstances might actually call a community to do so. For example, a parish which has been named in honor of St. Christopher and in which there is a deep devotion to the saint might search for appropriate ways in which to liturgically commemorate him. Likewise, certain "saints" who remain culturally prominent, such as St. Valentine and St. Nicholas, might need to be appropriately acknowledged in liturgical celebrations.

By way of another caution it should be noted that this principle does not and should not legitimate the forgetting and/or ignoring of the unknown and silent saints "who rest in unvisited tombs."

Universality. Those saints deemed important for the universal church are included in the universal calendar. The GNLYC, paragraph 9, states that "the saints of universal significance have celebrations obligatory throughout the entire Church. Other saints either are listed in the General Calendar for optional celebration or are left to the veneration of some particular Church, region, or religious family." At best this principle is somewhat ambiguous. It is difficult to determine which saints are truly of universal significance for the whole church. Any number of questions can be raised here. *Who* determines which saints are important? Who has been consulted in the process? Have both sexes and many nations been included? What general criteria ought to govern the determination of saintly witness which is of universal significance? What ideologies underpin the choices?

Despite the many problematic issues involved in applying this principle it did yield positive results in that a number of saints were

removed from the calendar. This helped unclutter seasonal liturgical cycles and it offered opportunities for the inclusion of saints who
were more significant to particular churches and communities.
Thus, saints who are not necessarily significant for the universal
church and yet who are significant to particular churches and communities (dioceses, religious orders, nations, or even continents)
were shifted or emerged in "particular calendars." For example, in
the dioceses of the United States, St. Elizabeth Ann Seton (January
4) is celebrated as significant because she is the first canonized
American-born saint.

Inclusivity. The sanctoral calendar ought to strive to be more
inclusive. A criticism which has been recently leveled against the
sanctoral cycle is that it tends to ignore certain groups. Prior to the
most recent reforms of the sanctoral cycle the saints included tended
to be representative of the following groups: White, European, hierarchy, members of religious orders, celibate, and male.

Recent reforms have tended toward a greater sensitivity to and
inclusion of other groups. There is, however, still a long way to go in
this matter. One factor which continues to contribute to this problem is the beatification/canonization process. The process is one
which demands financial resources, tight organization, and full-
time personnel. Some religious orders have these readily available
and can thus promote certain causes. Some revamping of the process is urgently needed!

Date. Where possible, the liturgical commemoration of a saint
ought to take place on the day of her or his death. The GNLYC
(#56) notes that "the Church's practice has been to celebrate the
saints on the date of their death ('birthday')." This rather traditional
practice is not meant to be morbid. Rather, in Christian tradition
the day of death was most usually thought to be the day of the saint's
true *natale,* or birth, into heaven. It was and is also tied into the
notion of the saint as a paschal witness. This is of special significance
in the case of martyrial celebrations.

Where it is not possible to do this (for example, because of
certain seasonal cycles, annual celebrations, feasts of the Lord, and
so forth) the celebration can be moved to some other appropriate date.

Ranking. Sanctoral celebrations abide by the categories of progressive solemnization: solemnity, feast, obligatory memorial, optional memorial. Generally speaking, solemnities, feasts, and obligatory memorials are to be celebrated. Optional memorials, as the name implies, are subject to pastoral decisions. All of these need not necessarily be celebrated; yet neither ought they all be ignored. It should probably be kept in mind that the greater number of sanctoral celebrations are going to be celebrated by a rather small portion of the parish community (since it is generally a small number of any parish community which celebrates daily eucharist, and few parishes celebrate the Liturgy of the Hours in common daily).

It seems appropriate, however, that communities invest some time and thought in consideration of the celebration of certain sanctoral days, whether this be the celebration of the saint under whose patronage a parish has been placed, or a culturally and/or ethnically significant saint (for example, St. Patrick in an Irish community). We need the witness of concrete persons from our tradition. The solidarity of the saints in Christ breaks through even the barrier of time and space.

PASTORAL ISSUES

The practice of liturgical commemorations of the saints raises a number of questions regarding certain pastoral issues and customs. The issues which will be entertained here are primarily those which impinge on liturgical practice (rather than extra-liturgical devotions).

Biography. Communities sometimes celebrate the memory of a saint while actually knowing nothing about the concrete circumstances of the saint's biography. The purpose of this section on "biography" is to offer a process for the preparation and inclusion of the biography of a saint within the framework of eucharistic liturgy or Liturgy of the Hours. Five basic steps are proposed as the components of this process. These steps are offered simply as one approach among many. There is a certain logic implicit in the sequence of these steps, but these allow for flexibility in terms of an alteration of the sequence.

1. Consult a *Lives of the Saints* in order to get some back-

ground regarding the specifics of the saint's biography. As was mentioned, communities sometimes observe certain sanctoral celebrations with little knowledge about even the barest sketch of the saint's life. It might be helpful to fill in this gap by incorporating a brief biography of the saint into the eucharistic liturgy and/or Liturgy of the Hours. This might be done in several ways—in a reading of the saint's life prior to the beginning, during the opening rite, or in the homily. (Certain editions of the Liturgy of the Hours books contain a brief biography of the saint being commemorated. This could serve as the basis for a biographical account.) When presented outside the homily, such a biography should be brief and simple.

2. Consult the "Office of Readings" in the Liturgy of the Hours book (if one is available). This often contains a writing from the saint who is being commemorated. Such writings can be helpful in that they assist the community in gaining a sense of the charism of the saint. Communities might want to explore ways in which such a reading might be incorporated into the liturgy in a responsible way. Such readings, however, should never replace the word of God.

3. Consult the liturgical prayer texts of the sanctoral cycle, especially the opening prayer of the eucharist. The sanctoral solemnities, feasts and memorials generally contain an opening prayer proper to the celebration. This prayer often highlights some particular aspect of the saint's life and gives some insight into the liturgical meaning of the specific sanctoral celebration. Also, the opening prayer often helps to bridge the connection between the concrete life of the saint and the paschal mystery. One should also consult other proper prayers where these are available (for example, the prayer over the gifts, the prayer after communion, and prefaces).

4. Consult the sanctoral lectionary (when specific readings are provided). These have been chosen in order to shed light on the meaning of the saint's life in the liturgical context. Such readings are obviously not provided for all the celebrations in the sanctoral cycle. When this is the case proper discernment ought to guide the choice of readings. In such cases it is important that the liturgical prayer texts as well as biographical material be consulted.

At this point there arises the question of the *lectio continua* (the usual two-year cycle of readings). As a general principle IT IS BEST

NOT TO INTRUDE ON THE *LECTIO CONTINUA.* Where possible the appointed readings from the *lectio continua* should be mined for their viability in any given sanctoral celebration. More often than not they are capable of sustaining the sanctoral celebration.

The concrete life of the saint and the scripture passages ought to shed light on one another. From a Catholic perspective there is no real antagonism between honoring the saints and preaching the gospel. Certainly the preaching of the gospel takes precedence over the honoring of the saints, but the saints are honored precisely because their lives were embodiments of the gospel. The saint *is* the gospel come to life in concrete circumstances. In the saint one can see, hear and touch the gospel. The saints express, not repress, the good news of Jesus Christ. Presiders, preachers, ministers, and planners of the liturgy might bear this in mind.

5. The community's needs and experiences must be consulted and discerned. In this regard several questions ought to be raised. a) What is the relationship between the particular community which is gathering for the liturgy and the particular saint who is being commemorated? For example, in many communities there exists a warm devotion to St. Francis of Assisi or St. Anthony of Padua. This relationship can become a cornerstone for building a deeper and more profound understanding of the communion of saints. If, on the other hand, there is no such prior relationship some questions might be raised as to whether or not a particular sanctoral commemoration needs to be celebrated (that is, where options are possible). b) Does the community need to hear some prophetic challenge from the concrete life of a saint (especially where no prior relationship may exist)? For example, does a particular community need to hear St. Vincent de Paul and St. Louise de Marillac challenging it regarding the quality of its outreach to the poor and abandoned? Does a community need to have St. Clare and St. Francis of Assisi challenge its consumerism? Thus, the warm devotion which a community may have for some saints needs at times to be put into tension with the prophetic, challenging dimensions of the same or other saints. Sometimes individuals and communities conveniently develop amnesia precisely because a saint's witness may be too uncomfortable. c) Finally, where options exist, who is responsible for deciding which

saints are and are not commemorated? Suffice it to say that such a judgment might best be made by all those who prepare the community's liturgical celebrations (rather than the presider alone).

To SUMMARIZE, then, in seeking to prepare for the celebration of sanctoral days, the following questions ought to be posed:

1. What is the LITURGICAL STATUS of the celebration: solemnity, feast, obligatory or optional memorial?

2. What is the BIOGRAPHY of the saint?

3. What do the WRITINGS of this saint tell us about her or him?

4. What do the LITURGICAL PRAYERS of the day offer as theological possibilities for understanding the celebration?

5. What are the LECTIONARY TEXTS and what possibilities do they offer for understanding the celebration?

6. What is the COMMUNITY'S RELATIONSHIP to the saint? What is the reason for the shape of that relationship? Is there a PROPHETIC dimension of the saint's life of which the community is in need?

7. What OTHER SOURCES are available for the celebration of the day (for example, music)?

The point in all this is that perhaps more energy ought to be channeled into the preparation for and celebration of certain sanctoral days. Preparation is often reduced to a consultation of lectionary texts. There are, however, other dimensions to be considered.

Music. The preparation of liturgical music for sanctoral celebrations is probably not going to be a complex process in most parishes and religious houses. Sanctoral days are generally neither solemnities nor feasts. They are usually not holy days of obligation and they are never celebrated on Sundays. Thus, the preparation of liturgical music for these days is usually a simple (and sometimes regrettably negligent) process. Keeping in mind the general guidelines for liturgical music, the following matters are noted.

Simplicity—Most sanctoral celebrations are ranked as obligatory or optional memorials. This ranking should be reflected in a certain simplicity regarding the amount and grandeur of the music.

Themes—"Thematizing" sanctoral celebrations through musical texts should be avoided. Themes are often ideologies of one sort or another in disguise. Liturgical celebration in honor of St. Vincent de Paul is a case in point. Vincent de Paul, of course, is well-known for his service to the poor. He is honored as the "universal patron of charity." Liturgical planners, however, might fall into the trap of searching out only those songs which explicitly speak about "serving the poor." These celebrations can run the risk of shifting the essential focus from praise of God to the need to serve the poor. That Christians may need to hear a prophetic challenge from St. Vincent de Paul to serve the poor is not questioned here; the problem is the mutation of liturgy into something essentially different which is caused by the aggressive infiltration of secondary ideologies.

Texts—The texts of the liturgical songs chosen for sanctoral celebrations should generally emphasize the triumph of God's grace and the presence of the paschal mystery in the life of the saint(s). Songs which actually mention by name the particular saint who is being liturgically commemorated certainly have a place in the liturgy. However, the broader context should be the praise of God and the centrality of the paschal mystery.

Some songs which honor individual saints are the remnants of a past era. As such, care must be taken when using these songs in liturgy (as well as in communal devotions). When the intercession of a particular saint is a dimension of a song's content, the notion of intercession should be imaged in a theologically responsible fashion. Furthermore, the intercession of a saint should not be the sole concern of a song.

This is not to suggest that traditional sanctoral hymns should not be used. It is simply to note that care should be taken in the choice of sanctoral songs.

Specificity—It is obviously not necessary to chase through hymnals and songbooks in search of songs which mention a particular saint. Such songs are difficult to come by these days. Every song used at a liturgical sanctoral celebration need not concern itself with a particular saint's holiness, and as a matter of fact, they need not even mention the saints. However, many songbooks and hymnals do contain general songs for the celebration of the "communion of saints."

General Guidelines—The guidelines for the selection of liturgical music in general apply here. Two other points might also be noted. First, consult the entrance and communion antiphons (if any) for the sanctoral celebrations. Particular antiphons can be found in the sacramentary for sanctoral celebrations of solemn, festal and obligatory memorial rankings. For sanctoral celebrations of the optional memorial ranking the particular "common" (for example, martyrs, pastors, and so forth) might be consulted. These antiphons are generally taken from scripture. For example, the entrance antiphon for the celebration of St. Justin (June 1) is: "The wicked tempted me with their fables against your law, but I proclaimed your decrees before kings without fear or shame" (see Psalm 118:85, 46). However, there are some which are non-scriptural and which make explicit mention of the particular saint. The entrance antiphon for the memorial in honor of St. Francis of Assisi (October 4) is an example of this: "Francis, a man of God, left his home and gave away his wealth to become poor and in need. But the Lord cared for him." These antiphons should give some insight into the tone of song texts for the gathering/entrance and communion songs. Second, there are times when songs in honor of saints are definitely inappropriate (for example, as a response to the first lectionary reading).

Devotions and Liturgy. As a general rule, the liturgy and sanctoral devotions should not be mingled. The liturgy is the official public prayer of the church. Devotions are by definition private (though they may take place in a communal context). The liturgy is not the place for novena prayers and other devotional practices in honor of individual saints.

For Personal Reflection and/or Group Discussion

1. Do you think that people living in the northern hemisphere/western world have lost a sense of memory of the dead? Do you think that people in our society believe in life beyond death? What examples (if any) can you think of which demonstrate our society's attempts to keep memory of the dead?

2. Do you ever invoke saints in your own prayer life? Which saints? Why? How do you invoke these saints?

3. Some have suggested that invocation of saints is characteristic of an immature and/or primitive faith? Do you agree?

4. Examine the prefaces for apostles, martyrs, pastors, virgins, and religious, holy men and women, and the feast of All Saints (P64-P71) in the sacramentary. What do these texts yield regarding a theology of holiness? Saints? Sanctoral feasts?

5. Examine the liturgical prayer texts for five or more sanctoral celebrations. What do these prayers say about the church's understanding of the liturgical commemoration of saints?

8

<hr>

Marian Celebrations

Her coming to birth
heralded joy and blessing for the whole world.
Her virgin-motherhood
brought forth the true Light,
the source of all joy.
Her hidden life
brings light and warmth
to the Church in every place.
Her passing into glory
raised her to the heights of heaven,
where, as our sister and our Mother,
she waits for us with loving care
until we too enjoy the vision of your glory for ever.
            PREFACE, THE BLESSED VIRGIN MARY,
                        CAUSE OF OUR JOY

THE CULT OF MARY: HISTORICAL BACKGROUND

The available historical evidence suggests that devotion to Mary was not a preoccupation of the various primitive Christian communities. However, the ***Protoevangelium of James*** (c. 150 C.E.) is an apocryphal work which concerns the life of Mary, and its existence suggests that there must have been some interest in the life of Mary even at this early date. This does not necessarily mean that there existed a cult in honor of Mary. In the third century is found the ***Praesidium*** prayer, a prayer to Mary which invokes her protection. However, the popularity of this prayer remains uncertain.

It is not until the Council of Ephesus (431 C.E.) that we have evidence of a strong devotion to Mary on any official level. Some writers, however, have suggested that the strength of this devotion (at least in Ephesus and its environs) is evidence that it actually predated Ephesus by several decades. At present there is no way of verifying that suggestion. What can be stated with certainty, is that Ephesus served as a catalyst to increase and strengthen the marian cult. Churches were built in Mary's honor and marian celebrations increased. The church in Rome celebrated a number of marian feasts by the late 600s. Among these were: Mary, Mother of God (January 1), the Purification of Mary (February 2), the Annunciation (March 25), and the Birth of Mary (September 8).

The tenth century experienced an explosion of marian devotion. Art, music, legends, relics, pilgrimages and miracles related to Mary abounded. The great marian prayers emerged at this time: the Hail Mary, the *Memorare,* the *Salve Regina,* the Rosary, and the *Angelus.*

During the Reformation period there was much criticism by both Protestant and Catholic reformers of certain marian exaggerations, and for a brief time the exaggerations were curbed. From the seventeenth century onward, however, marian devotion again exploded. The seventeenth through the twentieth centuries witnessed a number of marian apparitions (Rue de Bac, Lourdes, Fatima, and so forth) and a plethora of new marian devotional forms. The celebration of both apparitions and devotional titles came to be incorporated into the liturgy. It was also during this period that the doctrines of the Immaculate Conception (1854) and the Assumption (1950) became part of official Catholic teaching regarding Mary.

The Second Vatican Council sought to harness what had again become an exaggerated marian devotion. This led partly to the reform of marian liturgical celebrations.

MARIAN CELEBRATIONS IN THE LITURGICAL YEAR

The large number of marian celebrations in the liturgical year warrants giving special consideration to issues involved in the preparation of these liturgies. However, a word is first in order regarding the place of Mary in the GNLYC.

One of the few references to Mary in the GNLYC occurs in the section entitled "Solemnities, Feasts, and Memorials." It states that "the Church also venerates with a particular love Mary, the Mother of God, and sets before the devotion of the faithful, the memory of the martyrs and other saints" (para. 8). Two points of observation should be made. First, the GNLYC gives Mary a special place among the saints. Second (and perhaps even more significant), the document delineates the place of Mary as one among the saints. This is important precisely because there is a tendency at times to image and treat Mary as if she were another person within the Godhead.

The number and rankings of the various marian celebrations in the reformed calendar is as follows. The marian **solemnities** are: Mary, Mother of God (January 1), Assumption (August 15), and Immaculate Conception (December 8). (One should also mention here the Annunciation. However, in the reformed calendar the Annunciation is listed as a "feast of the Lord.") The marian *feasts* are: Visitation (May 31), the Birth of Mary (September 8), and Our Lady of Guadalupe (December 12, USA). The *obligatory memorials* are: Queenship of Mary (August 22), Our Lady of Sorrows (September 15), Our Lady of the Rosary (October 7), and the Presentation of Mary (November 21). There are also four *optional memorials:* Our Lady of Lourdes (February 11), Immaculate Heart of Mary (Saturday after the Solemnity of the Sacred Heart), Our Lady of Mount Carmel (July 16), and the Dedication of St. Mary Major (August 5).

A quick glance at the number and rankings of the various celebrations suggests several interesting insights. First, this ranking abides by a certain hierarchy of theological truths. Thus, those events which celebrate the central mysteries of Mary's life are given greater importance. All the marian celebrations are obviously not of equal value. Second, it is clear that greater significance is given those celebrations which are connected to *events* in the life of Mary. Finally, those celebrations which are of a *devotional* nature are generally ranked last (with the exception of the Guadalupe feast).

Further mention must be made of the fact that in the United States three of the six holy days of obligation are the three marian *solemnities.* Couple these marian holy days with the traditions of honoring Mary on Saturdays throughout the year (see GNLYC, para. 15), the Fourth Sunday of Advent, and during the months of

October and May, and one has the makings of a rather prominent marian veneration.

Time and space do not allow for an analysis of each one of these marian celebrations (see bibliography for books which do so). The general concern here is to note that there is a prominent tradition of marian devotion and to offer some general guidelines regarding preparation for these liturgical celebrations.

GENERAL PRINCIPLES

Liturgy. As the official public prayer of the church the liturgy is the ordinary and prominent means by which Mary is commemorated and honored. A question which is sometimes raised by both Catholics and Protestants is: Is devotion to Mary *required* for Catholic identity? The answer depends on how one understands "devotion." Since somewhat early times Mary has been honored in the public prayer of the church and thus, devotion to Mary does come with being a Catholic in the PUBLIC SENSE. Even now all of the approved eucharistic prayers mention Mary. However, while other pious marian devotions are recommended for Catholics, they are not of an obligatory nature.

Since the liturgy is the ordinary and prominent means by which we commemorate Mary and the mysteries of her life, great care should be taken in the preparation of liturgical celebrations which specifically honor Mary. For example, to prepare an elaborate communal rosary complete with scripture, drama and the rosary on the feast of the Assumption while the morning masses are dry, hurried and unsung is to reverse priorities.

In this process the liturgical rankings of marian celebrations should factor into the degree of elaboration with which a marian day is celebrated. This is not to suggest that on occasion lesser ranking celebrations will not be of a more festive nature. For example, communities of Mexican Americans may well celebrate the *feast* of Our Lady of Guadalupe (December 12) with far more festivity than the three marian *solemnities*/holy days. Generally speaking, however, liturgical rankings should be noted.

Texts. In liturgical celebrations honoring Mary, due consideration must be given to the prayer and scripture texts contained in the sacramentary and the lectionary. This is especially important with regard to marian celebrations, since these can inadvertently reflect a pious and devotional thrust which may have little to do with the actual liturgical celebrations. A close analysis of and adherence to the theology of marian celebrations as expressed in prayer and scripture texts might help communities to move away from overly sentimental and ideological approaches to celebrating and understanding such celebrations. Where possible it is helpful to explore the use of these prayers and scripture texts in educational programs and catechetical settings.

Devotion. A balanced and sensible approach to and appreciation for marian devotion ought to be maintained. Keeping in mind the priority of the liturgy, the cult of Mary as expressed in communal devotions ought not be ignored or eclipsed (except where such practices are clearly erroneous). Where such communal forms of devotion are appreciated and maintained *by members of the community* itself (that is, not imposed on them by a few individuals who have some particular devotion to some apparition, title, or practice) due consideration ought to be given them. There is a need for a healthy appropriation of such devotions which is cognizant of recent liturgical and theological shifts.

Paul VI, in his Apostolic Exhortation, ***Marialis Cultus*** noted a number of principles which ought to be applied when assessing devotion to Mary. First, the devotion must pay attention to theological integrity, that is, devotion to Mary must be contextualized within a proper theology of the Trinity, Christ, Spirit, and church. Second, devotion to Mary must have the scriptures as its wellspring. Third, devotion to Mary ought to be related to liturgy. Fourth, it must be cognizant and reflective of a sound anthropology. Finally, devotion to Mary must be ecumenically sensitive.

This concern for an appreciation of marian forms of devotion is not a license to confuse liturgy and private devotions, nor is it a legitimation of the practice of replacing liturgy with devotions (nor, for that matter, replacing devotions with liturgy). Both liturgy and private devotions can flourish in the life of a community and its individual members. This is a call to respect both liturgy and devotional forms as dimensions of the lives of Christians and to keep in mind the functions and dynamisms of both.

In this regard it is necessary to mention a practice which continues in some parishes and communities, that is, the incorporation of certain marian devotional prayers into the eucharistic liturgy. As a rule such devotional prayers by their nature should be prayed outside the framework of the liturgy. They are a matter of choice and should not be imposed on the broader community.

PASTORAL ISSUES

Music. Before dealing with the thorny question of *when* to sing a marian song in the liturgy, it is appropriate that the question of *what* to sing be addressed first. This is a matter of both text and music.

A number of marian songs which are questionable both in terms of theological propriety and musical quality continue to be used in liturgy. Great care and discernment must be taken in the selection of appropriate marian songs. Care and sound judgment must also be exercised in the textual adjustment of traditional marian songs and the composition of new songs in honor of Mary. In the case of a number of traditional marian songs the texts might be modified to reflect the church's present understanding of the person, image, and mystery of Mary. In still other cases the entire text of the song must be discarded and new texts composed.

Once again, the guidelines provided by Paul VI in **Marialis Cultus** should serve for the evaluation of texts of marian songs. Is the song rooted in scripture? (At a minimum the theology of the texts ought not be contrary to scripture.) Is there a theological integrity about the song? For example, does the song image Mary in a theologically correct and responsible manner? Do the texts image Mary in a sound human way (sound anthropology)? Are the texts of the song ecumenically sensitive or do they suggest an inflated "mariolatry"?

In many respects melodies prove to be as problematic as texts. On the one hand there are a number of new marian songs with melodies which are beautiful and quite appropriate for liturgy.

These songs should be mined and employed. On the other hand there are a number of marian songs of recent vintage which tend to be unusable for communities. The reasons for this are not easily determined. It may well be that in an effort to avoid the excessive sentimentality of some traditional marian songs, certain composers have unwittingly composed new ones which are cold and sterile.

These factors lead to two basic observations, especially for those who prepare the community's liturgy. First, care and caution must be exerted in trying to introduce new marian songs which may be theologically appropriate yet musically sterile. Second, discernment must be exercised regarding when and where to suppress traditional marian texts and melodies which have been lifegiving for a community.

This leads to some general principles which might be helpful. Where possible continue to sing traditional marian songs which have been and continue to be part of the community's tradition. Traditional marian songs which are neither excessively sentimental nor theologically inappropriate need not be discarded.

Also, retrieve melodies and texts where this is possible and desirable. For example, some of the great marian antiphons (*Ave Regina Caelorum, Alma Redemptoris Mater, Salve Regina, Ave Maria, Regina Caeli*) might be considered.

Third, alter problematic texts where this is possible. Where not, consider discarding the text entirely.

Fourth, as always, consult the entrance and communion antiphons of marian solemnities, feasts and memorials for a sense of the texts which might be sung at the time of the community's initial gathering and communion.

Liturgy of the Hours. Explore the possibility of praying the Liturgy of the Hours on certain marian days. The Liturgy of the Hours provides an alternative form of liturgical prayer with which a community can honor Mary. It might be desirable for a community to celebrate certain marian days (especially celebrations of local import) with the Liturgy of the Hours. From a practical point of view it might be difficult to do this in a large parish on certain marian holy days of obligation. However, on feasts and days of local popular marian celebration, evening prayer might be celebrated. Such alternative or additional celebrations can be significant especially as the prayer and scripture texts of the Liturgy of the Hours provide opportunities for deeper reflection on Mary.

For Personal Reflection and/or Group Discussion

1. There appears to have been a radical decrease in marian devotion since the close of the Second Vatican Council. What reasons would you offer for this decrease?

2. Many have suggested that devotion to Mary prior to the Second Vatican Council was too extreme. Some have even referred to it as "mariolatry." Do you think this was so? Why or why not?

3. Does Mary have a significant place in your own life? In the life of your community or parish? Why or why not?

4. Examine the opening prayers and the prefaces for the solemnities of Mary, Mother of God, the Immaculate Conception, and the Assumption. What image and theology of Mary do these present?

Summary

Quite a number of ideas have been presented throughout this book. The following are offered as brief summary statements to help appropriate the main ideas of this work:

1. The notion of a "liturgical year" is a fictive construct. While there is an integrity and unity to the liturgical year as a whole, it is probably more accurate to speak about a "cycle of feasts and seasons" which are celebrated by the church.

2. The *anamnesis* of the paschal mystery is the heart of all Christian liturgy. This paschal mystery is best understood as a supreme and dense disclosure of God's care for history which comes to focus in the life, passion, death and resurrection of Jesus Christ. The actualization of the saving events celebrated in *anamnesis* is one whereby we are drawn into those saving and redemptive events.

3. In the liturgical year we actualize saving events, not simply theological ideas.

4. The liturgical year is an *anamnesis* of saving events which entails both *bios* and *cosmos.* This *anamnesis* entails both word and sacrament/al. "Sacrament/al" entails the total symbolization life of the church.

5. Catholic Christians meet every week on the "Lord's day" to keep memory of Jesus Christ in word and sacrament. Eucharist and Sunday are intricately related.

6. The paschal triduum is to the liturgical year what Sunday is to the Christian week. It is the saving events clustered around *Pasch* which are celebrated.

7. The Lent-Easter-Pentecost cycle highlights the dynamics of passion/suffering/death/resurrection as these come to expression in **metanoia,** that is baptism, penance, reconciliation, conversion.

8. The Advent-Christmas-Epiphany cycle highlights the dynamics of incarnation/epiphany/manifestation. There is a dialectic here which appreciates the presence/absence, disclosure/concealment poles.

9. The sanctoral cycle is an anamnetic solidarity with those who have died and are now alive in God. Mary is of special significance among these. It entails canonized saints but also all who in death are alive in God. A certain respectful silence is at times due here.

10. There are a number of issues with which we need to continually grapple. Among these are: appropriate liturgical catechesis regarding the liturgical year, liturgical inculturation, and anamnesis and amnesia (especially regarding women's memories).

Seasons and Feasts Bibliography

A. GENERAL WORKS

Adam, Adolf. *The Liturgical Year: Its History and Its Meaning after the Reform of the Liturgy.* Translated by Matthew J. O'Connell. New York: Pueblo Publishing Company, 1981.

Barr, James. *Biblical Words for Time.* Great Britain: SCM Press, 1962.

Bosch, Paul. *Church Year Guide.* Minneapolis: Augsburg Publishing House, 1987. (Lutheran Tradition)

Buckland, Patricia B. *Advent to Pentecost: A History of the Christian Year.* Wilton: Morehouse-Barlow, 1979. (Episcopal Tradition)

The Calendar, Liturgy 1:2. Washington: The Liturgical Conference, 1980.

Carroll, Thomas K., and Thomas Halton (eds). *Liturgical Practice in the Fathers.* Wilmington: Michael Glazier, 1988.

Cullman, Oscar. *Christ and Time: The Primitive Christian Conception of Time and History.* Translated by Floyd V. Wilson. London: SCM Press, 1951.

Denis-Boulet, Noele M. *The Christian Calendar.* Translated by P. Hepburne-Scott. New York: Hawthorn Books, 1960.

Doerger, Berard. *I Am with You Always: Reflections on the Church Year.* Indiana: Our Sunday Visitor Publishing Division, 1988.

Dues, Greg. *Catholic Customs and Traditions: A Popular Guide.* Mystic: Twenty-Third Publications, 1989.

Hessel, Dieter T. (ed). *Social Themes of the Christian Year: A Commentary on the Lectionary.* Philadelphia: The Geneva Press, 1983.

Hickman, Hoyt, Don Saliers, Laurence Hull Stookey, and James F.

White. *Handbook of the Christian Year.* Nashville: Abingdon Press, 1986.

The Holy Cross, Liturgy 1:1. Washington: The Liturgical Conference, 1980.

Johnson, Lawrence J. (ed). *The Church Gives Thanks and Remembers: Essays on the Liturgical Year.* Collegeville: The Liturgical Press, 1984.

Kellner, K.A., Heinrich. *Heortology: A History of the Christian Festivals from Their Origin to the Present Day.* London: Kegan Paul, Trench and Co., 1908.

The Liturgical Year: Celebrating the Mystery of Christ and His Saints. Study Text 9. Washington: United States Catholic Conference, 1985.

Marchal, Michael. *Adapting the Liturgy: Creative Ideas for the Church Year.* San Jose: Resource Publications, 1989.

Martimort, A. G. (ed). *The Liturgy and Time (The Church at Prayer IV).* Translated by Matthew J. O'Connell. Collegeville: The Liturgical Press, 1986.

Martin, Gerhard Marcel. *Fest: The Transformation of Everyday.* Philadelphia: Fortress Press, 1976.

Mazar, Peter, Peter Scagnelli, and Fred Moleck. *Sourcebook for Sundays and Seasons: An Almanac of Parish Liturgy 19[91].* Chicago: Liturgy Training Publications, 19[90].

McArthur, A. Allan. *The Christian Year and Lectionary Reform.* London: SCM Press, 1958.

———. *The Evolution of the Christian Year.* Greenwich: The Seabury Press, 1953.

Nocent, Adrian. *The Liturgical Year,* 4 volumes. Translated by Matthew J. O'Connell. Collegeville: The Liturgical Press, 1977.

Otto, Eckart, and Tim Schramm. *Festival and Joy.* Translated by James L. Blevins. Nashville: Abingdon, 1980.

Porter, H. Boone. *Keeping the Church Year.* New York: The Seabury Press, 1977. (Episcopal Tradition)

Power, David (ed). *The Times of Celebration,* Concilium 142. New York: The Seabury Press, 1981.

Rochelle, Jay C. *The Revolutionary Year: Recapturing the Meaning of the Christian Year.* Philadelphia: Fortress Press, 1973.

Talley, Thomas. *The Origins of the Liturgical Year.* New York: Pueblo Publishing Company, 1986.

Vos, W. and G. Wainwright (eds). *Liturgical Time,* reprinted from *Studia Liturgica* 14 (1982).

Weiser, Francis X. *Handbook of Christian Feasts and Customs: The Year of the Lord in Liturgy and Folklore.* New York: Harcourt, Brace and World, 1952.

Wilde, James A. (ed). *At That Time: Cycles and Seasons in the Life of a Christian.* Chicago: Liturgy Training Publications, 1989.

B. SUNDAY/SABBATH AND "ORDINARY TIME"

Bacchiocchi, Samuele. *From Sabbath to Sunday: A Historical Investigation of the Rise of Sunday Observance in Early Christianity.* Rome: The Pontifical Gregorian Press, 1977.

Edwards, Tilden. *Sabbath Time: Understanding and Practice for Contemporary Christians.* New York: The Seabury Press, 1982.

Heschel, Abraham Joshua. *The Sabbath: Its Meaning for Modern Man*[sic]. New York: Farrar, Straus and Giroux, 1951.

Hurley, Karen (ed). *Why Sunday Mass? New Views for Those Who Go and Those Who Don't.* Cincinnati: St. Anthony Messenger Press, 1973.

Irwin, Kevin. *Sunday Worship: A Planning Guide to Celebration.* New York: Pueblo Publishing Company, 1983.

Kiesling, Christopher. *The Future of the Christian Sunday.* New York: Sheed and Ward, 1970.

The Lord's Day, Liturgy 8:1. Washington: The Liturgical Conference, 1981.

Millgram, Abraham E. *Sabbath: The Day of Delight.* Philadelphia: The Jewish Publication Society of America, 1944.

Porter, H. Boone. *The Day of Light: The Biblical and Liturgical Meaning of Sunday.* Washington: The Pastoral Press, 1960.

Searle, Mark (ed). *Sunday Morning: A Time for Worship.* Collegeville: The Liturgical Press, 1982.

C. LENT-EASTER-PENTECOST CYCLE

Boyer, Mark G. *Mystagogy: Liturgical Paschal Spirituality for Lent and Easter.* New York: Alba House, 1990.

Crichton, J. D. *Journey through Lent.* Rattlesden: Kevin Mayhew, 1989.

Easter's Fifty Days. Liturgy 3:1. Washington: The Liturgical Conference, 1982.

Franke, Hermann. *Lent and Easter: The Church's Spring.* Translated by the Benedictines of St. John's Abbey. Westminster: The Newman Press, 1979.

Hartgen, William E. *Planning Guide for Lent and Holy Week.* Glendale: Pastoral Arts Associates of North America, 1979.

Irwin, Kevin. *Easter: A Guide to the Eucharist and Hours.* Collegeville: The Liturgical Press, 1991.

———. *Lent: A Guide to the Eucharist and Hours.* Collegeville: The Liturgical Press, 1985.

Onley, Dan F. *The Great Sunday: Fifty Days of Easter in Your Parish.* Old Hickory: Pastoral Arts Associates of North America, 1983.

———. *Preparing for Lent: Resources and Priorities.* Old Hickory: Pastoral Arts Associates of North America, 1982.

Ryan, Vincent. *Eastertime and Feasts of the Lord.* Dublin: Veritas Publications, 1977.

Simcoe, Mary Ann (ed). *Parish Path through Lent and Eastertime.* Chicago: Liturgy Training Publications, 1985.

D. PASCHAL TRIDUUM/"HOLY WEEK'

Berger, Rupert, and Hans Hollerweger (eds). *Celebrating the Easter Vigil.* Translated by Matthew J. O'Connell. New York: Pueblo Publishing Company, 1983.

Bouyer, Louis. *The Paschal Mystery: Meditations on the Last Three Days of Holy Week.* Translated by Mary Benoit. Chicago: Henry Regnery Company, 1950.

Davies, J. Gordon. *Holy Week: A Short History.* Richmond: John Knox Press, 1963.

Fitzpatrick, Gerard, John H. Fitzsimmons, Robert B. Kelly, Patrick Taylor, and Anne Tiffney. *Focus on Holy Week: Pastoral Notes and Practical Suggestions.* Suffolk: Kevin Mayhew Publishers, 1986.

Freeman, Eileen (ed). *The Holy Week Book.* San Jose: Resource Publications, 1979.

Gaillard, Jean. *Holy Week–Easter.* Translated by William Busch. Collegeville: The Liturgical Press, 1954.

Huck, Gabe. *The Three Days: Parish Prayer in the Paschal Triduum.* Chicago: Liturgy Training Publications, 1981.

———, and Mary Ann Simcoe (eds). *A Triduum Sourcebook.* Chicago: Liturgy Training Publications, 1983.

Martin, John T. *Christ Our Passover: The Liturgical Observance of Holy Week.* London: SCM Press, 1958.

Neumann, Don A. *Holy Week in the Parish.* Collegeville: The Liturgical Press, 1991.

Pelton, Robert D. *Circling the Sun: Meditations on Christ in Liturgy and Time.* Washington: The Pastoral Press, 1986.

Ramshaw, Gail. *Words Around the Fire: Reflections on the Scriptures of the Easter Vigil.* Chicago: Liturgy Training Publications, 1990.

Shepherd, Massey H. *The Paschal Liturgy and the Apocalypse.* Richmond: John Knox Press, 1960.

Stevenson, Kenneth. *Jerusalem Revisited: The Liturgical Meaning of Holy Week.* Washington: The Pastoral Press, 1988.

Tyrer, John Walton. *Historical Survey of Holy Week: Its Services and Ceremonial.* London: Oxford University Press, 1932.

E. ADVENT-CHRISTMAS-EPIPHANY CYCLE

Advent-Christmas-Epiphany, Liturgy 4:3. Washington: The Liturgical Conference, 1984.

Days of the Lord: The Liturgical Year 1 (Advent, Christmas, Epiphany). Collegeville: The Liturgical Press, 1991.

Fitzpatrick, Gerard. *Focus on Advent and Christmas: A Programme of Pastoral Notes, Practical Suggestions and Music.* Suffolk: Kevin Meyhew Publishers, 1986.

Griffin, Eltin (ed). *Celebrating the Season of Advent.* Dublin: The Columba Press, 1986.

Irwin, Kevin W. *Advent and Christmas: A Guide to the Eucharist and Hours.* Collegeville: The Liturgical Press, 1986.

Onley, Dan. *Planning Parish Worship for Advent and Christmas.* Old Hickory: Pastoral Arts Associates of North America, 1982.

Simcoe, Mary Ann (ed). *Parish Path through Advent and Christmastime.* Chicago: Liturgy Training Publications, 1983.

F. SANCTORAL CYCLE

Perham, Michael. *The Communion of Saints: An Examination of the Place of the Christian Dead in the Belief, Worship, and Calendars of the Church.* London: Alcuin Club, 1980.

With All the Saints, Liturgy 5:2. Washington: The Liturgical Conference, 1985.

G. MARIAN CELEBRATIONS

O'Donnell, Christopher. *At Worship with Mary.* Wilmington: Michael Glazier, 1988.

H. "HOLY DAYS"

Holy Days in the United States: History, Theology, Celebration. Washington: United States Catholic Conference, 1984.

Holy Days: Opportunities and Challenges. Ottawa: Canadian Conference of Catholic Bishops, 1985.

I. CATECHESIS/RELIGIOUS EDUCATION

Halmo, Joan. *Celebrating the Church Year with Young Children.* Collegeville: The Liturgical Press, 1988.

Nelson, Gertrud Mueller. *To Dance with God: Family Ritual and Community Celebration.* New York: Paulist Press, 1986.

Westerhoff, John H. *A Pilgrim People: Learning Through the Church Year.* Minneapolis: Augsburg Publishing House, 1962.

J. TIME

Fagg, Lawrence W. *Two Faces of Time.* Wheaton: The Theosophical House, 1985.

Hall, Edward T. *The Dance of Life: The Other Dimension of Time.* New York: Doubleday, 1983.

K. LITURGY OF THE HOURS

Batiffol, Pierre. *History of the Roman Breviary.* Translated by Atwell Baylay. New York: Longmans, Green and Company, 1912.

Baudot, Dom. *The Breviary: Its History and Contents.* Translated by the Benedictines of Stanbrook. St. Louis: B. Herder Book Company, 1929.

Beckwith, Roger T. *Daily and Weekly Worship: From Jewish to Christian.* Bramcote: Grove Books Limited, 1987.

Bradshaw, Paul F. *Daily Prayer in the Early Church.* London: SPCK, 1981.

Cutts, David, and Harold Miller. *Whose Office? Daily Prayer for the People of God.* Bramcote: Grove Books, 1982.

Dugmore, C.W. *The Influence of the Synagogue upon the Divine Office.* Westminster: The Faith Press, 1964.

Flannery, Austin (ed). *Companion to the New Breviary.* Costello Publishing Company.

Gallen, John (ed). *Christians at Prayer.* Notre Dame: University of Notre Dame Press, 1977.

Guiver, George. *Company of Voices: Daily Prayer and the People of God.* New York: Pueblo Publishing Company, 1988.

Hoornaert, Rodolphe. *The Breviary and the Laity.* Collegeville: The Liturgical Press, 1936.

Jeremias, Joachim. *The Prayers of Jesus.* Philadelphia: Fortress Press, 1967.

Jungmann, Joseph A. *Christian Prayer Through the Centuries.* Translated by John Coyne. New York: Paulist Press, 1978.

The Liturgy of the Hours (Study Text 7). Washington: NCCB, 1981.

Liturgy: Rhythms of Prayer (Journal of the Liturgical Conference 8/4). Washington: The Liturgical Conference, 1990.

Martimort, A. G. *The Liturgy and Time (The Church at Prayer IV).* Translated by Matthew J. O'Connell. Collegeville: The Liturgical Press, 1986.

Quigley, E.J. *The Divine Office: A Study of the Roman Breviary.* M.H. Gill and Son, 1930.

Roguet, A. M. *The Liturgy of the Hours: The General Instruction with Commentary.* Collegeville: The Liturgical Press, 1971.

Salmon, Dom Pierre. *The Breviary Through the Centuries.* Translated by Sister David Mary. Collegeville: The Liturgical Press, 1962.

Scotto, Dominic F. *Liturgy of the Hours: Its History and Importance As the Communal Prayer of the Church After the Liturgical Reform of Vatican II.* Petersham: St. Bede's Publications, 1987.

Taft, Robert. *The Liturgy of the Hours in East and West: The Origins of the Divine Office and Its Meaning for Today.* Collegeville: The Liturgical Press, 1986.

Index

Actions: of Lent-Easter-Pentecost,
77–78, 93; *See also* Symbols
Advent-Christmas-Epiphany:
Advent wreath use, 121–123;
Christmas crèche use, 123–
125; colors for, 119–121;
dynamism of, 114–115; and
fixed calendar, 6; historical
background, 102–105; in
liturgical year, 105–107, 115–
118; music for, 125–130; and
outside celebrations, 109–110;
parameters for, 106–107, 161;
and paschal mystery, 110–111;
theological focus for, 118–119;
See also Christmas
Agape, and eucharist, 41
Agriculture: and early feasts, 25;
and ember days, 65–66
All Souls liturgy, and personal
saints, 140
Almsgiving, 81; *See also* Penance
Amnesia, in liturgical celebration,
15–16
Anamnesis: and communal
memory, 10; feminist, 38; of
paschal mystery, 92–93, 160
Anniversaries, in personal
calendars, 6

Annunciation. *See* Solemnity of
the Annunciation
Arts: in liturgical celebration, 36–
37; women in, 39; *See also*
Music
Ascension: in Easter celebration,
74; historical observance of,
68–69
Ash Wednesday, 71, 73, 75;
pastoral issues for, 78–79;
prayer for, 76, 81; *See also*
Lent-Easter-Pentecost
Astronomy: in calendar reform, 28;
See also Cosmic events

Baptism, 72, 74, 88; and
community, 15; and Lent, 69–
70; and reconciliation, 74; *See
also* Initiation;
Lent-Easter-Pentecost
Baptism of the Lord: and
Epiphany, 106, 107; feast of, 12
Beatification. *See* Canonization
Biography of Christ, and liturgical
year, 14
Biological time: and cosmic
rhythms, 6; *See also* Time
Birthdays, in personal calendars, 6